Ace your Maths exams with CGP!

Let's face it, National 5 Maths is seriously challenging. You can't just stroll into the exams with your lucky pencil and hope for the best — you're going to need plenty of practice to make sure you're ready.

That's where this brilliant CGP book comes in. It's jam-packed with challenging exam-style questions for every topic, all rounded off with a full set of practice papers that are just like the real SQA exams.

We've also included fully-worked answers at the back, so if you drop any marks, it's easy to find out exactly where you went wrong.

CGP — the best by miles! ☺

Our sole aim here at CGP is to produce the highest quality books — carefully written, immaculately presented and dangerously close to being funny.

Then we work our socks off to get them out to you — at the cheapest possible prices.

D1493000

Published by CGP

Editors:
Tom Miles, Alison Palin, Dave Ryan, Caley Simpson

With thanks to Shaun Harrogate and Ian MacAndie for the proofreading.

ISBN: 978 1 78294 944 2

Clipart from Corel®
Printed by Elanders Ltd, Newcastle upon Tyne

Based on the classic CGP style created by Richard Parsons.

Contents

How to Use This Book.................................... 2
Exam Tips..3
Reasoning Skills..4

Section One — Numerical Skills

Fractions...5
Percentages...6
The Laws of Indices....................................9
Scientific Notation....................................10
Manipulating Surds....................................12

Section Two — Algebraic Skills

Expanding Brackets...................................13
Factorising...15
Solving Equations......................................16
Inequalities..18
Rearranging Formulas................................19
Functions...21
Straight Line Graphs..................................22
Factorising Quadratics...............................24
The Quadratic Formula...............................25
Completing the Square................................26
Quadratic Graphs......................................27
Sketching Quadratic Graphs........................29
The Discriminant.......................................30
Algebraic Fractions...................................31
Simultaneous Equations.............................32

Section Three — Geometric Skills

Geometry...34
Polygons..35
Circle Geometry..37
Similarity...39
Arcs and Sectors.......................................41
Volume..43
Pythagoras' Theorem.................................45
3D Coordinates...48
Vectors..49

Section Four — Trigonometric Skills

Trigonometric Graphs.................................51
Trigonometry — Sin, Cos, Tan....................52
Related Angles..53
Solving Trig Equations................................54
Trig Identities...56
The Sine and Cosine Rules..........................57
Trigonometry with Bearings........................59

Section Five — Statistical Skills

Comparing Data Sets..................................60
Scattergraphs...62

Practice Papers

Practice Paper 1..64
Practice Paper 2..75

Answers...88
Formula Sheet...102

How to Use This Book

Hold the book <u>upright</u>, approximately <u>50 cm</u> from your face, ensuring that the text looks like <u>this</u>, not s̄ɪɥʇ.
Alternatively, place the book on a <u>horizontal</u> surface (e.g. a table or desk) and sit adjacent to the book,
at a distance which doesn't make the text too small to read.

In case of emergency, press the two halves of the book together <u>firmly</u> in order to close.

Before attempting to use this book, familiarise yourself with the following <u>safety information</u>:

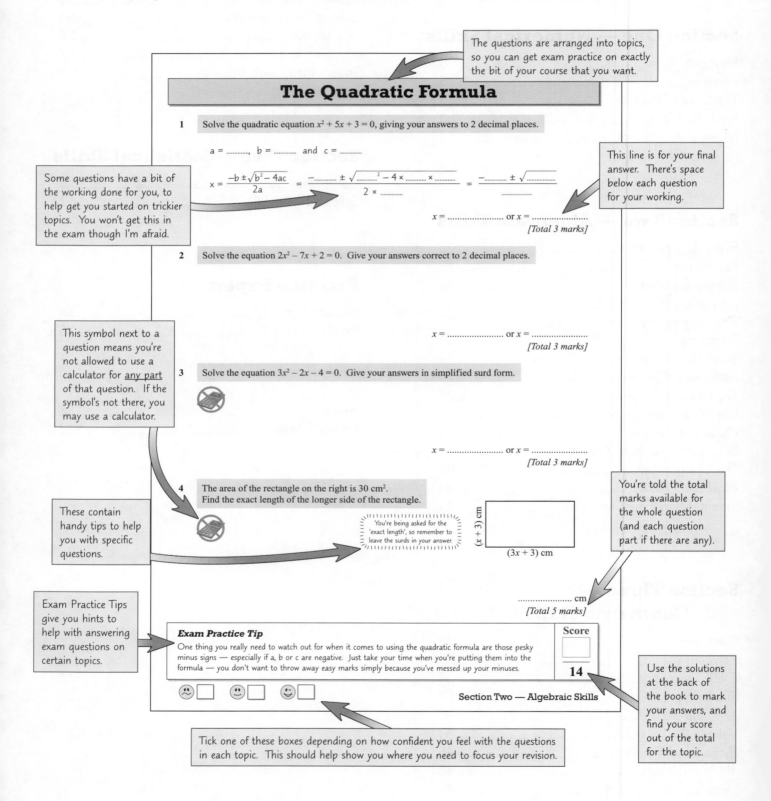

The questions are arranged into topics, so you can get exam practice on exactly the bit of your course that you want.

The Quadratic Formula

1   Solve the quadratic equation $x^2 + 5x + 3 = 0$, giving your answers to 2 decimal places.

a = ...,   b = ...   and   c = ...

Some questions have a bit of the working done for you, to help get you started on trickier topics. You won't get this in the exam though I'm afraid.

$$x = \frac{-b \pm \sqrt{b^2 - 4ac}}{2a} = \frac{-......... \pm \sqrt{.........^2 - 4 \times .... \times ....}}{2 \times ....} = \frac{-......... \pm \sqrt{.........}}{.........}$$

This line is for your final answer. There's space below each question for your working.

$x = $ .... or $x = $ ....
[Total 3 marks]

2   Solve the equation $2x^2 - 7x + 2 = 0$. Give your answers correct to 2 decimal places.

$x = $ .... or $x = $ ....
[Total 3 marks]

This symbol next to a question means you're not allowed to use a calculator for <u>any part</u> of that question. If the symbol's not there, you may use a calculator.

3   Solve the equation $3x^2 - 2x - 4 = 0$. Give your answers in simplified surd form.

$x = $ .... or $x = $ ....
[Total 3 marks]

These contain handy tips to help you with specific questions.

4   The area of the rectangle on the right is 30 cm². Find the exact length of the longer side of the rectangle.

You're being asked for the 'exact length', so remember to leave the surds in your answer.

$(x + 3)$ cm

$(3x + 3)$ cm

You're told the total marks available for the whole question (and each question part if there are any).

.... cm
[Total 5 marks]

Exam Practice Tips give you hints to help with answering exam questions on certain topics.

Exam Practice Tip

One thing you really need to watch out for when it comes to using the quadratic formula are those pesky minus signs — especially if a, b or c are negative. Just take your time when you're putting them into the formula — you don't want to throw away easy marks simply because you've messed up your minuses.

Score

14

Use the solutions at the back of the book to mark your answers, and find your score out of the total for the topic.

☹ ☐   ☺ ☐   ☺ ☐

Section Two — Algebraic Skills

Tick one of these boxes depending on how confident you feel with the questions in each topic. This should help show you where you need to focus your revision.

Exam Tips

Exam Stuff

1) You will have <u>two</u> exams — one <u>non-calculator</u> exam and one <u>calculator</u> exam.

2) The non-calculator exam is <u>1 hr 15 mins</u> long and worth <u>50 marks</u>.

3) The calculator exam is <u>1 hr 50 mins</u> long and worth <u>60 marks</u>.

4) Timings in the exam are really important, so here's a quick guide...

> • You should spend roughly 1-1.5 minutes per mark working on each question (i.e. 2 marks = 2-3 minutes).
>
> • Then, if you've got any time left at the end of the exams, check back through your answers and make sure you haven't made any silly mistakes. Don't just stare at that hottie in front.
>
> • If you're totally, hopelessly stuck on a question, just leave it and move on to the next one. You can always go back to it at the end if you've got enough time.

There are a Few Golden Rules

1) **Always, always, always make sure you <u>read the question properly</u>.**
For example, if the question asks you to give your answer in metres, <u>don't</u> give it in centimetres.

2) **Show <u>each step</u> in your <u>working</u>.**
You're less likely to make a mistake if you write things out in stages. And even if your final answer's wrong, you'll probably pick up <u>some marks</u> if the examiner can see that your <u>method</u> is right.

3) **Check that your answer is <u>sensible</u>.**
Worked out an angle of 450° or 0.045° in a triangle? You've probably gone wrong somewhere...

4) **Make sure you give your answer to the right <u>degree of accuracy</u>.**
The question might ask you to round to a certain number of <u>significant figures</u> or <u>decimal places</u>. So make sure you do just that, otherwise you'll almost certainly lose marks.

5) **Look at the number of <u>marks</u> a question is worth.**
If a question's worth 2 or more marks, you're not going to get them all for just writing down the final answer — you're going to have to <u>show your working</u>.

6) **Write your answers as <u>clearly</u> as you can.**
If the examiner can't read your answer you won't get any marks, even if it's right.

> Obeying these Golden Rules will help you get as many marks as you can in the exam — but they're no use if you haven't learnt the stuff in the first place. So make sure you revise well and do <u>as many</u> practice questions as you can.

Using Your Calculator

1) Your calculator can make questions a lot easier for you but only if you <u>know how to use it</u>. Make sure you know what the different buttons do and how to use them.

2) Remember to check your calculator is in <u>degrees mode</u>. This is important for <u>trigonometry</u> questions.

3) If you're working out a <u>big calculation</u> on your calculator, it's best to do it in <u>stages</u> and use the <u>memory</u> to store the answers to the different parts. If you try and do it all in one go, it's too easy to mess it up.

4) If you're going to be a renegade and do a question all in one go on your calculator, use <u>brackets</u> so the calculator knows which bits to do first.

> REMEMBER: <u>Golden Rule number 2</u> still applies, even if you're using a calculator — you should still write down <u>all</u> the steps you are doing so the examiner can see the method you're using.

Reasoning Skills

Reasoning skills are all about how you tackle a mathematical problem and explain the answer.
You'll have to use reasoning skills on both exam papers, so it's a good idea to know what you need to do.

There are Two Main Types of Reasoning Questions...

1) For some questions, it's <u>obvious</u> what you have to do — e.g. 'solve the equation $x^2 + 5x + 6 = 0$'
   is clearly a question on <u>quadratic equations</u>, so solve it using the usual methods.

2) However, in other questions, it's <u>not obvious</u> what you have to do — you're given some <u>information</u>,
   and have to work out what <u>methods</u> to use to answer the question. These questions are designed to
   assess how you approach an <u>unfamiliar problem</u> — they test your <u>reasoning skills</u>.

3) Reasoning questions come in <u>two different forms</u> —
   in both cases, you have to work out what maths to do <u>for yourself</u>.

Questions With a Real-Life Context

1) If questions have a <u>real-life context</u>, the information you need might be <u>hidden</u> in all the wordiness.
   You need to read through the question and work out which bits are <u>relevant</u> to the maths,
   and which bits are just <u>setting the scene</u>.

2) Once you've worked this out, decide which <u>method(s)</u> you need to use to answer the question.
   After doing all your <u>calculations</u>, make sure you <u>link</u> your answer back to the <u>original context</u>.

3) It can be pretty obvious what maths you need to use, even with a real-life context —
   <u>scientific notation</u> and <u>simultaneous equations</u> are often given in context.
   Sometimes it's <u>not</u> that obvious though — which leads us nicely onto...

Sometimes questions will be a mixture of both — i.e. problem-solving questions set in a real-life context.

Problem-Solving Questions

1) In <u>problem-solving questions</u>, you'll be given a load of <u>mathematical information</u>
   (sometimes including <u>diagrams</u>) and asked to '<u>calculate</u>' or '<u>find</u>' a certain value.
   It's then up to you to come up with a <u>strategy</u> to answer the question.

2) You won't be given any <u>guidance</u> for what method to use — you have work it out for yourself.

3) There are often a couple of <u>different ways</u> you could answer the question — and you'll get the marks
   whichever way you do it, as long as you get the <u>answer</u> right and <u>show your working</u> clearly.

Here are Some Useful Tips for Reasoning Questions

Unfortunately, there's <u>no</u> one set method for answering reasoning questions — they can be on anything
the examiners fancy, so will involve <u>different bits</u> of maths. These <u>tips</u> should help you get started though.
Don't forget the Golden Rules from the previous page. They all still apply to reasoning questions —
especially rules 2) and 3).

- <u>Read the question</u> two or three times and work out what you're <u>trying to find</u>.
- Write down what you <u>know</u> — pick out any <u>numbers</u> given in the question, and add <u>labels</u> to
  diagrams if you can. If you're not given a diagram, it's often a good idea to <u>sketch one yourself</u>.
- See if anything <u>jumps out</u> at you — for example, <u>right-angled triangles</u> might mean you need to
  use <u>Pythagoras</u> or <u>trigonometry</u>, or <u>squared terms</u> might mean you're working with a <u>quadratic</u>.
- <u>Don't rush</u> into a problem-solving question — <u>take your time</u> and <u>think it through</u> first.
  Make sure you have an <u>idea</u> of what you're going to do before diving in.

Fractions

1 Evaluate $4\frac{2}{5} + 3\frac{1}{4}$.

....

[Total 2 marks]

2 Work out the value of $2\frac{5}{6} - 1\frac{1}{5}$.

Give your answer in its simplest form.

....

[Total 2 marks]

3 Evaluate $4\frac{3}{5} \times 2\frac{1}{3}$.

....

[Total 2 marks]

4 Work out the value of $4\frac{1}{3} \div 2\frac{3}{5}$.

Give your answer in its simplest form.

....

[Total 2 marks]

5 Evaluate $\frac{3}{8}\left(1\frac{2}{5} - \frac{4}{3}\right)$.

....

[Total 2 marks]

6 Evaluate the calculation below.

$$7\frac{1}{5} - 2\frac{1}{4} \times 2\frac{1}{3}$$

....

[Total 3 marks]

Score:

13

Percentages

1 A computer costs £927 plus VAT, where VAT is charged at 20%.
Find the total cost of the computer.

£ ....
[Total 2 marks]

2 A conservation company plants pine trees in a forest to increase their number.
During 2014, the number of pine trees increased by 12%.
During 2015, the number of pine trees increased by a further 8%.

At the start of 2014 there were 5000 pine trees in the forest.
How many pine trees were there in the forest at the end of 2015?

....
[Total 3 marks]

3 In a rugby stadium, 90% of the seats are full. There are 54 000 people in the seats.

Calculate the total number of seats in the stadium.

54 000 = 90%

54 000 ÷ .... = ... = ...%

.... × .... = 100% = ...

....
[Total 3 marks]

4 After an 8% pay rise Mr Brown's salary was £15 714.

What was his salary before the increase?

£ ....
[Total 3 marks]

5   Amy is 12.5% taller than she was a year ago. She is now 135 cm tall.

How tall was she a year ago?

.... cm

[Total 3 marks]

6   A caravan has dropped 30% in value. It is now worth £11 549.

What was its original value to the nearest pound?

£ ....

[Total 3 marks]

7   The population of fish in a lake is estimated to decrease by 8% every year.

Approximately how many fish will be left after 15 years if the initial population is 2000?
Give your answer to the nearest whole number of fish.

Population after 15 years = 2000 × (1 − ....)⁻⁻⁻

= 2000 × (..............)⁻⁻⁻

= ....

....

[Total 3 marks]

8   Mrs Burdock borrows £750 to buy a sofa.
She is charged 6% interest per annum.

Per annum just means per year.

If Mrs Burdock doesn't pay back any of the money for 3 years, how much will she owe?
Give your answer to the nearest penny.

£ ....

[Total 3 marks]

Section One — Numerical Skills

9 Mrs Khan puts £2500 into a high interest savings account, which has an interest rate of 4.5%. Interest is added to the account at the end of each year, and she doesn't take any money out or put any more money into the account.

How much money will there be in Mrs Khan's account after 4 years?
Give your answer to the nearest penny.

£ ....

[Total 3 marks]

10 A new house cost £135 000, but increased in value by 15% each year.

Work out its value after 5 years, to 3 significant figures.

£ ....

[Total 3 marks]

11 A car dealership is selling a used car. The car was worth £15 000 when new and its value has decreased by 11% each year.

After how many years will the car be worth less than half its original value?

> Work out what half the original value will be, then use trial and error to find how long it takes for the value to fall below this amount.

....

[Total 3 marks]

Exam Practice Tip

Once you've got your answer, compare it to the value given in the question and see if it seems sensible. If it's a percentage <u>increase</u> question, you'd expect the answer to be <u>bigger</u> than the original value, but if it's a percentage <u>decrease</u>, you'd expect it to be <u>smaller</u>. If it's not, something's gone wrong somewhere.

Score

32

Section One — Numerical Skills

The Laws of Indices

1   Evaluate 5^{-2}.

....
[Total 1 mark]

2   Evaluate $16^{\frac{3}{4}}$.

   $16^{\frac{3}{4}} = (16^{\frac{1}{4}})^3 = (\ldots\ldots\ldots)^3 = \ldots\ldots\ldots$

....
[Total 2 marks]

3   For values of $y \geq 2$, write the following expressions in order from smallest to largest.

$$y^{-3} \qquad y^3 \qquad y^1 \qquad y^0 \qquad y^{\frac{1}{3}}$$

....
[Total 2 marks]

4   Write $\dfrac{5x^3}{\sqrt{x}}$ in the form mx^n, where m and n are constants.

....
[Total 2 marks]

5   Simplify $5a^{\frac{3}{2}} \times \left(2a^{\frac{5}{2}}\right)^3$.

....
[Total 3 marks]

6   Simplify $\dfrac{12n^{13}}{2n \times 3n^4}$.

....
[Total 3 marks]

Score:

13

Section One — Numerical Skills

Scientific Notation

1 Light travels at approximately 1.86×10^5 miles per second.
The distance from the Earth to the Sun is approximately 9.3×10^7 miles.

How long will it take light to travel this distance?
Give your answer in scientific notation.

.... seconds
[Total 2 marks]

2 The distance from Neptune to the Sun is approximately 4.5×10^9 km.
The distance from the Earth to the Sun is approximately 1.5×10^8 km.

Calculate how many times greater the distance from Neptune to the Sun is than the distance from the Earth to the Sun.

....
[Total 3 marks]

3 The maximum speed of a race car's engine is 1.2×10^4 RPM (revolutions per minute).
To test the engine's durability for a race, it is run at full speed for 2 hours.

How many revolutions will the engine make during the test?
Give your answer in scientific notation.

....
[Total 2 marks]

4 A cake recipe needs 150 g of sugar.
On average, one grain of sugar has a mass of 2×10^{-4} g.

How many grains of sugar are used in the cake?
Give your answer in scientific notation.

....
[Total 3 marks]

5 A patient has been prescribed a dose of 4×10^{-4} grams of a certain drug to be given daily.

a) The tablets that the hospital stocks each contain 8×10^{-5} grams of the drug.
How many tablets should the patient be given each day?

....

[3]

b) The doctor increases the patient's daily dose of the drug by 6×10^{-5} grams.
What is the patient's new daily dose of the drug?
Give your answer in scientific notation.

TIP: you need matching powers
to be able to add two numbers
together in scientific notation.

.... grams per day

[3]

[Total 6 marks]

6 An underwater gas pipeline is cylindrical, with a diameter of 1.06 m.
The pipeline is 1.05×10^6 m long.

Calculate the volume of the pipeline.
Give your answer in scientific notation, correct to 2 significant figures.

.... m^3

[Total 3 marks]

7 A cruise ship has a mass of approximately 7.59×10^7 kg.
Its passengers have a total mass of 2.1×10^5 kg.

Express the mass of the passengers as a percentage of the total combined
mass of the ship and passengers. Give your answer to 2 significant figures.

.... %

[Total 3 marks]

Exam Practice Tip	Score
Questions on scientific notation can be a bit confusing — it's not always clear whether you should multiply or divide, so read the question carefully. Also take care to give your answer in the correct form — an answer in scientific notation has to be in the form $A \times 10^n$, where $1 \leq A < 10$, and you might have to round as well.	
	22

Section One — Numerical Skills

Manipulating Surds

1 Write $2\sqrt{50} - (\sqrt{2})^3$ in the form $a\sqrt{b}$, where a and b are integers.

[Total 3 marks]

2 Express $\dfrac{6}{\sqrt{20}}$ as a fraction with a rational denominator.

 Give your answer in its simplest form.

[Total 3 marks]

3 Express $\sqrt{99} + \dfrac{22}{\sqrt{11}}$ in the form $a\sqrt{11}$, where a is an integer.

[Total 3 marks]

4 Express $\dfrac{6 + \sqrt{8}}{\sqrt{2}}$ in the form $a\sqrt{2} + b$, where a and b are integers.

[Total 4 marks]

Score:

13

Section One — Numerical Skills

Expanding Brackets

1   Expand $5a(3a + 6ab)$.

....

[Total 1 mark]

2   Expand and simplify $3p(8 - p) - 4p(2p - 7)$.

....

[Total 2 marks]

3   Expand and simplify $4a^2(2a - 5) + a(3a + 4a^2)$.

....

[Total 2 marks]

4   Multiply out the brackets and collect like terms: $(4t - 3)(2t + 5)$.

....

[Total 2 marks]

5   Expand and simplify $(2x + 9)^2$.

....

[Total 2 marks]

6 Show that the area of the triangle below can be written as $x^2 + 2x - 3$.

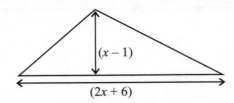

[Total 3 marks]

7 Expand and simplify $(2x + 3)(x^2 - 2x + 2)$.

[Total 3 marks]

8 Look at the cuboid below.

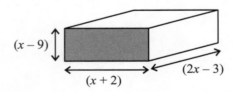

a) Find an expression for the area of the shaded face.
   Expand and simplify your expression.

[2]

b) Find an expression for the volume of the cuboid.
   Give your answer in the form $ax^3 + bx^2 + cx + d$.

[3]

[Total 5 marks]

Exam Practice Tip

If you're struggling with double brackets, don't forget you can always use the <u>FOIL</u> method — multiply the <u>F</u>irst term in each bracket together, then multiply the <u>O</u>utside terms together, then the <u>I</u>nside terms, and finally multiply together the <u>L</u>ast term in each bracket... easy.

Score

20

Factorising

1 Factorise fully $7y - 21y^2$.

$$7y - 21y^2 = 7(\text{............} - \text{............}) = 7\text{......} (\text{............} - \text{............})$$

....
[Total 1 mark]

2 Factorise fully $2v^3w + 8v^2w^2$.

....
[Total 1 mark]

3 Factorise $x^2 - 16$.

....
[Total 1 mark]

4 Factorise $9n^2 - 4m^2$.

....
[Total 1 mark]

5 Factorise fully $3y^2 - 27$.

....
[Total 2 marks]

Score:

6

Section Two — Algebraic Skills

Solving Equations

1   Solve the equation $\frac{5}{4}(2c - 1) = 3c - 2$.

$c = $ ....

[Total 3 marks]

2   Find x such that $\frac{8 - 2x}{3} + \frac{2x + 4}{9} = 12$.

$x = $ ....

[Total 3 marks]

3   The diagram below shows an equilateral triangle.

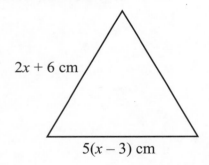

$2x + 6$ cm

$5(x - 3)$ cm

Find the length of one side of the equilateral triangle.

.... cm

[Total 4 marks]

4 The quadrilateral below has a perimeter of 58 cm.

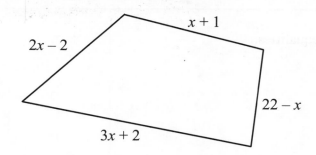

All of the lengths on this diagram are in cm.

Find the value of x.

$x =$ ....

[Total 3 marks]

5 The diagram below shows two rectangles.
Rectangle A has sides of length $2x + 3$ cm and $5x - 8$ cm.
Rectangle B has sides of length $3x + 6$ cm and y cm.

5x − 8 cm

2x + 3 cm	Rectangle A

3x + 6 cm

Rectangle B	y cm

a) Rectangle B has the same perimeter as rectangle A.
Write an equation for y in terms of x.

....

[3]

b) The perimeter of each rectangle is 32 cm. Find the value of y.

$y =$ ....

[3]

[Total 6 marks]

Exam Practice Tip

It's a good idea to check your solutions by substituting them back into the equation and checking that everything works out properly. It certainly beats sitting and twiddling your thumbs or counting sheep for the last few minutes of your exam.

Score

19

Section Two — Algebraic Skills

Inequalities

1   Solve the following inequalities.

a) $6q - 8 < 40$

....

[2]

b) $\dfrac{3x}{4} \leq 9$

....

[2]

[Total 4 marks]

2   Solve algebraically the following inequalities.

a) $7x - 2 < 2x - 42$

....

[2]

b) $9 - 4x > 17 - 2x$

....

[2]

[Total 4 marks]

3   Solve algebraically the inequation $4 - 2p \leq 2p + 5$.

....

[Total 2 marks]

4   Solve the inequality $13x + 3 \geq 3(5 - x)$.

....

[Total 3 marks]

5   Solve the inequality $-x < 9x + 2(x - 1)$.

....

[Total 3 marks]

Score:

16

Rearranging Formulas

1 Neela is on holiday in New York. The local weather forecast gives the temperature in °F. Neela wants to know what this temperature is in °C.

The formula for converting temperatures in °C to °F is: $F = \frac{9}{5}C + 32$.
Rearrange the formula to make C the subject.

$$F = \frac{9}{5}C + 32 \quad \text{so} \quad \frac{9}{5}C = F - \text{............} \quad \text{and}$$

$$C = \frac{\text{........}}{\text{........}}(\text{..........................})$$

....

[Total 2 marks]

2 A result used in physics is $P = \frac{V^2}{R}$, where P is the power in watts (W), V is the voltage in volts (V) and R is the resistance in ohms (Ω).

a) Change the subject to R.

$$\frac{v^2}{R} = P$$

$$R = \frac{P}{v^2}$$

....

[2]

b) Change the subject to V.

$$\frac{v^2}{R} = P \qquad v^2 = P^{\bullet}$$

$$v = \sqrt{pr}$$

....

[1]

[Total 3 marks]

3 The formula for the displacement, s, of a dropped object in free fall is $s = \frac{1}{2}gt^2$, where g is the constant acceleration due to gravity and t is time taken.

Rearrange the formula to make t the subject.

....

[Total 3 marks]

4 The relationship between a, b and y is given by the formula $a + y = \frac{b - y}{a}$.

Rearrange the formula to make y the subject.

....

[Total 4 marks]

Functions

1 f is a function such that $f(x) = \dfrac{3}{2x + 5}$.

 Find f(7.5)

....
[Total 2 marks]

2 f and g are functions such that $f(x) = 2x^2 + 3$ and $g(x) = \sqrt{2x - 6}$.

 a) Find f(9)

....
[2]

b) Find g(21)

....
[2]

c) Solve g(a) = 0.

....
[3]

[Total 7 marks]

3 A function is defined as $h(x) = \dfrac{5}{\sqrt{x - 1}}$.

 Express h(11) as a fraction in its simplest form with a rational denominator.

....
[Total 2 marks]

4 The function f(x) is defined by $f(x) = \sqrt{x^2 - 25}$.

 a) Evaluate f(13).

....
[2]

b) Given that f(c) = 2, calculate the possible values of c.

....
[3]

[Total 5 marks]

Score:

16

Section Two — Algebraic Skills

Straight Line Graphs

1 A straight line has equation $4y - 5x = 8$.

a) Find the gradient of the line.

$4y = 5x + 8$

$y = \dfrac{5}{4} + 2$

$m = \dfrac{5}{4}$ or 1.25

....
[2]

b) State the coordinates of the point where the line crosses the y-axis.

$(0, 2)$

....
[1]

[Total 3 marks]

2 Line **L** passes through the points $(0, -3)$ and $(5, 7)$, as shown below.

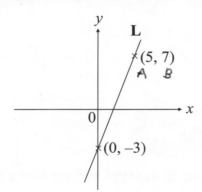

a) Find the equation of line **L**.
Give the equation in its simplest form.

$\dfrac{y^2 - y^1}{x^2 - x^1} = \dfrac{7 - -3}{5 - 0}$ $\dfrac{10}{5} = 2$

$y - b = m(x - a)$

$y - 7 = 2(x - 5)$

$y - 7 = 2x - 10$

$\underline{y = 2x - 3}$

....
[3]

b) Find the equation of the line which is parallel to line **L**
and passes through the point $(2, 10)$.

A B

$y - b = m(x - a)$

$y - 10 = 2(x - 2)$

$y - 10 = 2x - 4$

$y = 2x + 6$

....
[2]

[Total 5 marks]

3   The graphs of two lines are sketched below. The equation of line A is $3x + 5y = 15$.

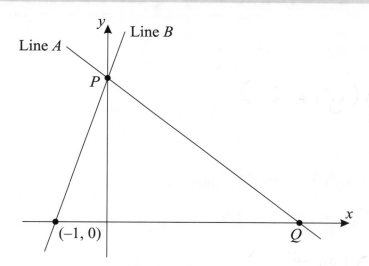

a)   Find the gradient of line A.

$$y = -\frac{3}{5} + 3$$

....

[2]

b)   Find the coordinates of point Q.

when $y = 0, 3x = 15$
  so $x = 5$

$Q(\underline{5}, \underline{0})$

[1]

c)   Given that both lines pass through point P on the y-axis, find the equation of line B.

$3(0) + 5y = 15$ $y = mx + c$
$y = 3$ $y = 3x + 3$
$$\frac{(3 - 0)}{(0 - -1)}$$
$$\frac{3}{1} = 3$$

....

[3]

[Total 6 marks]

4   Find the equation of the line which passes through the points $(-1, 17)$ and $(5, -7)$.

  A   B

Give your answer in the form $y = mx + c$.

$$\frac{-7 - 17}{5 - -6}$$ $y = mx$
$$\frac{-24}{6}$$ $y - b = m(x - a)$
        $y - -7 = m4(x-5)$
-4 $y + 7 = -4x + 20$
        $y = -4x + 13$

....

[Total 3 marks]

Score: $\boxed{17}$

$\overline{17}$

Section Two — Algebraic Skills

Factorising Quadratics

1 Factorise the quadratic $y^2 + 2y - 24$.

$$(y - 4)(y + 6)$$

....

[Total 1 mark]

2 The function $f(x) = 3x^2 - 13x - 10$ is a quadratic.

a) Fully factorise $f(x)$.

$$(3x + 2)(x - 5)$$

....

[2]

b) Hence, solve $f(x) = 0$.

$x =$ .... or $x =$ ....

[1]

[Total 3 marks]

3 The shape on the right is made from a square and a triangle.

The sides of the square are $(x + 3)$ cm long and the height of the triangle is $(2x + 2)$ cm. The area of the whole shape is 60 cm².

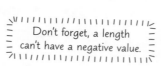 Don't forget, a length can't have a negative value.

a) Show that $x^2 + 5x - 24 = 0$.

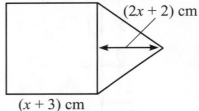
$(2x + 2)$ cm

$(x + 3)$ cm

[3]

b) Find the value of x.

$x =$ ....

[3]

[Total 6 marks]

Exam Practice Tip

In the exam, you can check that you've factorised an expression properly by expanding the brackets back out. You should get the expression that you started with. If you don't then something must have gone wrong somewhere down the line and you'll need to give it another go. Sorry about that.

Score

10

Section Two — Algebraic Skills

The Quadratic Formula

1   Solve the quadratic equation $x^2 + 5x + 3 = 0$, giving your answers to 2 decimal places.

$a =$ ...., $b =$ ....   and $c =$ ....

$$x = \frac{-b \pm \sqrt{b^2 - 4ac}}{2a} = \frac{-............ \pm \sqrt{............^2 - 4 \times .... \times ....}}{2 \times ....} = \frac{-............ \pm \sqrt{............}}{............}$$

$x =$ .... or $x =$ ....

[Total 3 marks]

2   Solve the equation $2x^2 - 7x + 2 = 0$. Give your answers correct to 2 decimal places.

$x =$ .... or $x =$ ....

[Total 3 marks]

3   Solve the equation $3x^2 - 2x - 4 = 0$. Give your answers in simplified surd form.

$x =$ .... or $x =$ ....

[Total 3 marks]

4   The area of the rectangle on the right is 30 cm².
Find the exact length of the longer side of the rectangle.

> You're being asked for the 'exact length', so remember to leave the surds in your answer.

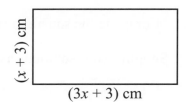
$(x + 3)$ cm

$(3x + 3)$ cm

.... cm

[Total 5 marks]

Exam Practice Tip

One thing you really need to watch out for when it comes to using the quadratic formula are those pesky minus signs — especially if a, b or c are negative. Just take your time when you're putting them into the formula — you don't want to throw away easy marks simply because you've messed up your minuses.

Score

14

Section Two — Algebraic Skills

Completing the Square

1 Given that $x^2 + ax + b = (x + 2)^2 - 9$, work out the values of a and b.

$a =$ .... and $b =$ ....

[Total 2 marks]

2 Write the expression $x^2 - 8x + 6$ in the form $(x + a)^2 + b$.

....

[Total 2 marks]

3 The expression $x^2 - 10x - 5$ can be written in the form $(x + p)^2 + q$.

 a) Find the values of p and q.

$p =$ .... and $q =$ ....

[2]

b) Use your answer to solve the equation $x^2 - 10x - 5 = 0$.
Leave your answer in surd form.

$x =$ .... or $x =$ ....

[1]

[Total 3 marks]

4 Complete the square to find the exact solutions to the equation $x^2 + 20x + 56 = 0$.

Simplify your solutions as far as possible.

$x =$ .... or $x =$ ....

[Total 4 marks]

Exam Practice Tip

Completing the square is pretty tough stuff. If you're struggling to get your head around it, just remember... when the quadratic expression is in the form $x^2 + bx + c$, the number in the brackets is always $b \div 2$ and the number outside the brackets is always $c - (b \div 2)^2$.

Score

11

Quadratic Graphs

1   The diagram on the right shows part of the graph of $y = nx^2$.

Find the value of n.

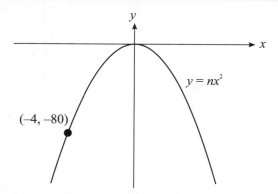

$y = nx^2$

$(-4, -80)$

$n =$ ....

[Total 2 marks]

2   A cannon fires a cannonball into the air.
The path of the cannonball follows the parabola $y = -(x + r)^2 + s$.

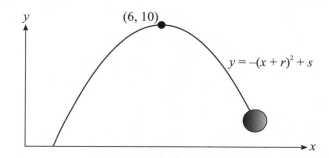

$(6, 10)$

$y = -(x + r)^2 + s$

The cannonball is at its highest at the point $(6, 10)$.

a)   State the value of r.

$r =$ ....
       [1]

b)   State the value of s.

$s =$ ....
       [1]

c)   Give the equation of the axis of symmetry of the parabola.

....
       [1]

d)   Write the equation of the parabola in the form $y = ax^2 + bx + c$.

....
       [2]

[Total 5 marks]

Section Two — Algebraic Skills

3 A parabola with equation $y = (x + p)^2 + q$ is sketched below.

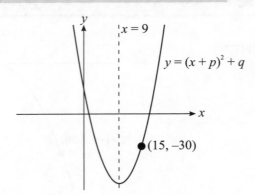

The axis of symmetry of the parabola is the line $x = 9$.
The point $(15, -30)$ lies on the parabola.

a) Write down the value of p.

$p = $ ....
[1]

b) Determine the value of q.

$q = $ ....
[2]

c) State the coordinates of the turning point of the parabola.

(.............. , ...)
[1]

[Total 4 marks]

4 Find the coordinates of the turning point of the graph of $f(x) = x^2 - 4x + 6$.

(.............. , ...)
[Total 3 marks]

Score: ☐

14

Section Two — Algebraic Skills

Sketching Quadratic Graphs

1   Sketch the graph of $y = (x + 2)^2 + 20$.

On your sketch, clearly show the coordinates of the
turning point and the point of intersection with the y-axis.

[Total 3 marks]

2   Sketch the graph of $y = x^2 + 10x - 11$, showing the coordinates of the
turning point and any points where the curve intersects the axes.

[Total 4 marks]

Exam Practice Tip

To get all the marks in a sketching question, you'll have to make sure you show all the important bits of
information — it's not enough to just get the shape right. The turning point and y-intercept will usually be
asked for and the x-intercepts might also be needed, especially if the quadratic can be easily factorised.

Score

7

The Discriminant

1   Determine the nature of the roots of the quadratic equation $y = 10x^2 - 14x + 2$.

....

[Total 2 marks]

2   The function f(x) is defined by f(x) = $9x^2 + 6x + 1$.

Determine whether the graph of y = f(x) intersects the x-axis and, if so, how many times.

....

[Total 2 marks]

3   The quadratic f(x) = $2x^2 + kx + k$ has one real, repeated root.

Given that $k \neq 0$, use the discriminant to find the value of k.

Discriminant = ... − (......... × .... × ....) = ... − ....

One real, repeated root $\Rightarrow$ Discriminant = 0

So .... = 0 $\Rightarrow$ ....(......... − ....) = 0

$\Rightarrow$ k = ... or k = ...   k = ...

[Total 3 marks]

4   Determine the values of p for which the equation $x^2 + 4x + p = 0$ has no real solutions.

....

[Total 4 marks]

Exam Practice Tip

It might be tempting to hide under your exam desk and hope a discriminant question doesn't find you, but there's no escaping these questions — so learn the formula for the discriminant and what it tells you about the nature of the roots. And remember, remember, remember — use the proper language.

Score

11

Algebraic Fractions

1   Simplify $\dfrac{x^2 - 4}{x^2 + 8x + 12}$.

....
[Total 3 marks]

2   Express $\dfrac{x^2}{3x} \times \dfrac{6}{x+1}$ $(x \neq 0, x \neq -1)$ as a single fraction in its simplest form.

....
[Total 2 marks]

3   Express $\dfrac{10x}{3+x} \div \dfrac{4}{5(3+x)}$ $(x \neq -3)$ as a single fraction in its simplest form.

....
[Total 3 marks]

4   Write $\dfrac{2}{3} + \dfrac{m-2n}{m+3n}$ as a single fraction.

$$\frac{2}{3} + \frac{m-2n}{m+3n} = \frac{2 \times \text{............}}{3 \times \text{............}} + \frac{\text{......} \times (m-2n)}{\text{......} \times (m+3n)} = \frac{2\text{............} + \text{......}(m-2n)}{\text{......}(m+3n)}$$

$$= \frac{\text{............}}{\text{............}} = \frac{\text{............}}{\text{............}}$$

....
[Total 3 marks]

5   Write $\dfrac{1}{x-5} + \dfrac{2}{x-2}$ $(x \neq 2, x \neq 5)$ as a single fraction in its simplest form.

....
[Total 3 marks]

Score:

14

Section Two — Algebraic Skills

Simultaneous Equations

1   Solve algebraically the system of equations:

$x + 3y = 11$
$3x + y = 9$

$x = $ .... $y = $ ....
[Total 3 marks]

2   Solve algebraically the pair of simultaneous equations:

$2x + 3y = 12$
$5x + 4y = 9$

$x = $ .... $y = $ ....
[Total 3 marks]

3   A sweet shop sells bags of pick 'n' mix. A bag that contains
4 chocolate frogs and 3 sugar mice costs £3.69.

a)   Write down this information as an equation.

....
[1]

b)   A bag that contains 6 chocolate frogs and 2 sugar mice costs £3.96.
Write down this information as an equation.

....
[1]

c)   Calculate the cost of one chocolate frog and the cost of one sugar mouse.

Chocolate frog: ....

Sugar mouse: ....
[4]

[Total 6 marks]

Section Two — Algebraic Skills

4 The diagram shows the graphs of $y = 18 - 3x$ and $y = 2x - 2$.

a) Find the coordinates of point P.

....

[2]

b) Find the coordinates of point Q.

....

[2]

[Total 4 marks]

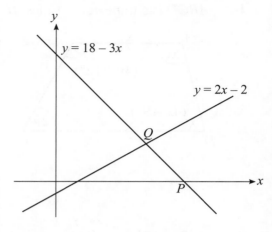

5 The graph shows two straight lines. Their equations are below.

$$3x + 5y = 49$$
$$5x + 2y = 31$$

The lines intersect at the point R.
Determine the coordinates of point R algebraically.

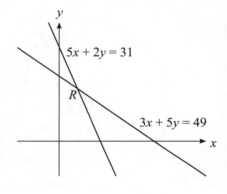

....

[Total 3 marks]

6 Solve algebraically the system of equations:

$$3y - 4 = 5(x - 2) \text{ and } 3x = 2y + 5$$

$x = $ .... $y = $ ....

[Total 4 marks]

Exam Practice Tip

When you're solving simultaneous equations in the exam, it's always a good idea to check your answers at the end. Just substitute your values for x and y back into the original equations and see if they add up as they should. If they don't then you must have gone wrong somewhere, so go back and check your working.

Score

23

Section Two — Algebraic Skills

Geometry

1 ABCD is a trapezium. Lines AB and DC are parallel to each other.

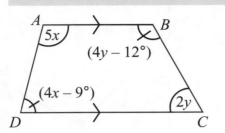

Find the values of x and y.

If you extend the lines in the diagram, it might be easier to see how to solve the problem.

x = ... °   y = ... °

[Total 4 marks]

2 A, B and C are points on a circle, centre O. OA, OB and OC are radii of the circle. OBD is a straight line and EF is the tangent to the circle at A. Angle OCB = 27° and angle FDB = 142°.

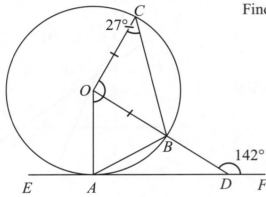

Find the size of angle AOC. Show your working clearly.

OBC = OCB = ... °

So COB = ... ° – .... ° – .... ° = ...

ADO = ... ° – .... ° = ...

OAD = ... °

So AOD = ... ° – .... ° – .... ° = ...

Then AOC = ... ° + ... ° = ... °

..................°

[Total 3 marks]

3 AGF and BD are parallel lines. AEDC and BEG are straight lines.

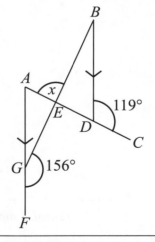

Work out the size of angle x.

..................°

[Total 3 marks]

Exam Practice Tip

If you find yourself staring at a geometry problem in the exam not knowing where to start, just try finding any angles you can — don't worry tooooo much at first about the particular angle you've been asked to find. Just make sure you make it really clear which angle you're finding at each step. Label the diagram if it helps.

Score

10

Polygons

1 *ABCD* is a kite. Line *DX* is the same length as line *AD*.

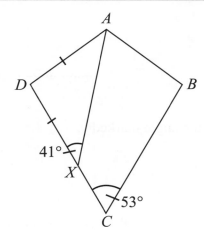

Find the size of angle *DAB*.

..............°

[Total 3 marks]

2 Part of a regular polygon is shown below. Each interior angle is 150°.

 Calculate the number of sides of the polygon.

....

[Total 2 marks]

3 The diagram shows a regular pentagon and an equilateral triangle.

Work out the size of the angle *p*.

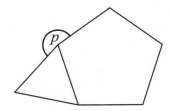

..........................°

[Total 3 marks]

4 The diagram shows a regular octagon. *AB* is a side of the octagon and *O* is its centre.

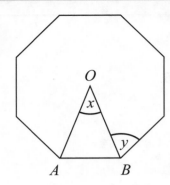

a) Work out the size of the angle marked *x*.

x = ...°

[2]

b) Work out the size of the angle marked *y*.

y = ...°

[2]

[Total 4 marks]

5 *ABCDEF* is an irregular hexagon and *G* is a point on line *CD*.
AB, *FG* and *ED* are parallel lines.

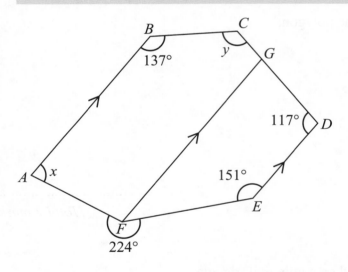

Find the size of:

a) angle *x*

x = ...°

[3]

b) angle *y*

y = ...°

[2]

[Total 5 marks]

Exam Practice Tip

You need to know the number of sides of a regular polygon to work out its interior and exterior angles —
so make sure you've swotted up on the different types of polygon. Altogether now: equilateral triangle (3),
square (4), pentagon (5), hexagon (6), heptagon (7), octagon (8), nonagon (9), decagon (10).

Score

17

Circle Geometry

1   *A* and *C* are points on the circumference of the circle with centre *O*.
BD is the tangent to the circle at *C* and angle *ACD* = 53°.

Find the size of angle *AOC*.

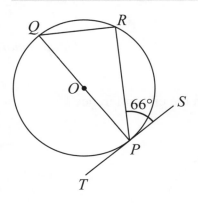

.................................°

[Total 2 marks]

2   The diagram below shows a circle, centre *O*. *P*, *Q* and *R* are points on the
circumference of the circle. *SPT* is a tangent to the circle. Angle *RPS* is 66°.

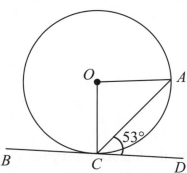

Find the size of angle *PQR*.

.................................°

[Total 2 marks]

3   The diagram below shows a circle with centre *O*. *ABC* and *ADE* are
tangents to the circle and *DOF* is a straight line. Angle *OFB* = 62°.

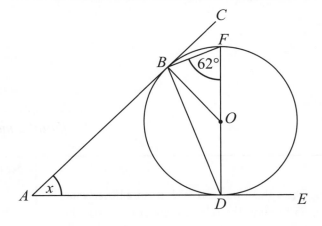

Work out the size of the angle marked *x*.

x = ...°

[Total 3 marks]

4   The points *A*, *B* and *C* lie on the circumference of a circle.
       BD and *AE* are straight lines which intersect at point *C*.
       The angle *DCE* is a right-angle and the angle *ABC* is 37°.

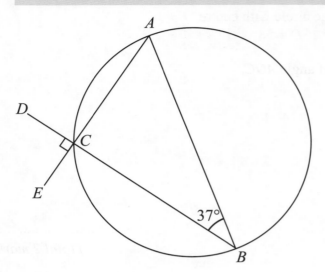

a)   Find the size of angle *BAC*.

....
                                                                [2]

b)   Explain why the line *AB* must pass
       through the centre of the circle.

                                                                [1]
                                                    [Total 3 marks]

5   The diagram shows a circle with centre *O*. *A* and *B* are points on the circumference.
       AC and *BC* are tangents to the circle. Angle *BDO* is 24°.

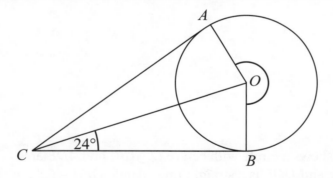

       Find the size of the reflex angle *AOB*.

....
                                                    [Total 3 marks]

Exam Practice Tip

Make sure you know the rules about circles really, really well. Draw them out and stick them all over your
bedroom walls, your fridge, even your dog. Then in the exam, go through the rules one-by-one and use them
to fill in as many angles in the diagram as you can. Keep an eye out for sneaky isosceles triangles too.

Score

13

Section Three — Geometric Skills

Similarity

1   The diagram below shows two similar triangles, **A** and **B**.
The length of the base of each triangle is given.

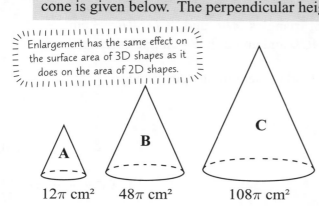

The area of triangle **B** is 6 cm².
Calculate the area of triangle **A**.

.... cm²
[Total 3 marks]

2   **A**, **B** and **C** are three solid cones which are mathematically similar. The surface area of each
cone is given below. The perpendicular height of **A** is 4 cm. The volume of **C** is 135π cm³.

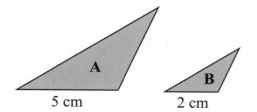

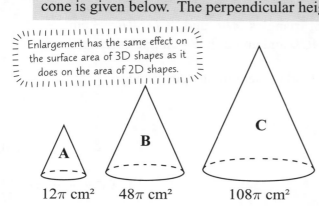

12π cm² 48π cm² 108π cm²

a)   Calculate the volume of **A**.

Scale factor from **A** to **C**:

n^2 = ... ÷ .... = ... $\Rightarrow$ n = ...

Volume of **A** = ... ÷ .... = ...

.... cm³
[3]

b)   Calculate the perpendicular height of **B**.

.... cm
[3]

[Total 6 marks]

3   Two mathematically similar banners are shown below.

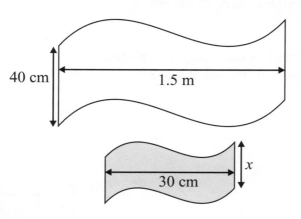

a)   What is the length, in cm, of *x*?

.... cm
[2]

b)   The area of the unshaded banner is 0.6 m².
What is the area of the shaded banner?

.... m²
[2]

[Total 4 marks]

Section Three — Geometric Skills

4   *ABE* and *CDE* are similar triangles.

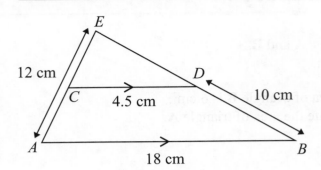

a)   Find the length of *CE*.

.... cm
[2]

b)   Find the length of *ED*.

.... cm
[2]

[Total 4 marks]

5   The quadrilateral *ABCD* is made up of two similar triangles, *ABC* and *ACD*. *AB* = 3 cm, *AD* = 8 cm and *AC* = 6 cm. Angle *ABC* = angle *ACD* and angle *ACB* = angle *CAD*.

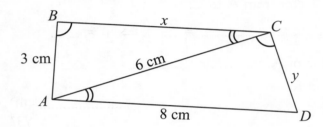

a)   Find the length of sides *x* and *y*.

x = ... cm

y = ... cm
[3]

b)   The area of triangle *ABC* is 9 cm². Determine the area of quadrilateral *ABCD*.

.... cm²
[2]

[Total 5 marks]

6   The cost of a box of rabbit feed is proportional to the volume of the box.

A shop sells two mathematically similar boxes.
The smaller box has a height of 40 cm and the larger box has a height of 50 cm.
The price of the larger box is £10. Calculate the price of the smaller box.

£ ....
[Total 3 marks]

Score:

25

Arcs and Sectors

1   Look at the sector shown in the diagram below.

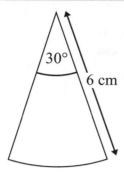

a)   Find the area of the sector.
      Give your answer to 3 significant figures.

.... cm²

[3]

b)   Find the perimeter of the sector.
      Give your answer to 3 significant figures.

.... cm

[3]

[Total 6 marks]

2   A circle, centre O, is split into a minor and major sector.

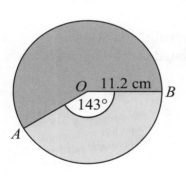

The radius of the circle is 11.2 cm
and the obtuse angle AOB is 143°.

Find the area of the major sector.
Give your answer to 1 decimal place.

.... cm²

[Total 3 marks]

3   A slice in the shape of a sector is taken from a cake, as shown below.

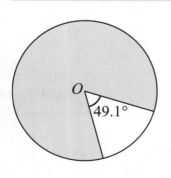

The angle of the removed slice is 49.1°
and the length of the arc is 10.3 cm.

Determine the diameter of the cake, to the nearest cm.

.... cm

[Total 3 marks]

Section Three — Geometric Skills

4   A torch company's logo is shown below.

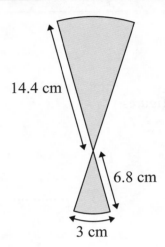

14.4 cm

6.8 cm

3 cm

The logo consists of the sectors of two circles centred at the same origin. The sectors are mathematically similar.

The larger circle has a radius of 14.4 cm and the smaller circle has a radius of 6.8 cm. The smaller sector has an arc length of 3 cm.

Calculate the area of the logo, giving your answer to 3 significant figures.

.... cm²

[Total 5 marks]

5   An industrial rolling machine is made up of three identical cylinders of radius 9 cm. The ends of the rollers are surrounded by a strip of metal, as illustrated in the diagram below.

Find the length of the metal strip, giving your answer correct to 1 d.p.

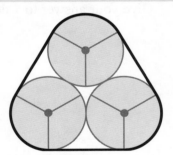

If you're struggling with the straight bits, try looking at the horizontal part first.

.... cm

[Total 4 marks]

Exam Practice Tip

Know the formulas for the length of an arc and the area of a sector and you've got this section in the bag — so long as you're also confident at rearranging them. You don't want to be left stumped if the exam asks you to find the angle or the radius. And don't make the age-old mistake of mixing up diameter and radius: d = 2r.

Score

21

Section Three — Geometric Skills

Volume

1 The diagram below shows Amy's new paddling pool.
It has a diameter of 2 metres, and is 40 cm high.

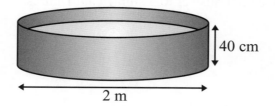

40 cm

2 m

The instructions that came with the pool say that it should only be filled three-quarters full.
What is the maximum volume of water that Amy can put in the pool?
Give your answer to 2 decimal places.

.... m³

[Total 3 marks]

2 The cross-section of a prism is a regular hexagon.

Each side of the hexagon has a length of 8 cm.
The distance from the centre of the hexagon to
the midpoint of each side is 7 cm.
Calculate the volume of the prism.

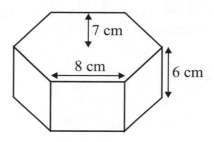

.... cm³

[Total 3 marks]

3 The cone and sphere in the diagram below have the same volume.

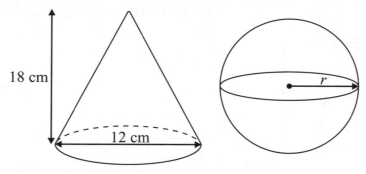

18 cm

12 cm

The cone has a vertical height of 18 cm and a base diameter of 12 cm.
Work out the radius, *r*, of the sphere. Give your answer to 3 significant figures.

.... cm

[Total 4 marks]

Section Three — Geometric Skills

4 The diagram below shows a wooden spinning top made from a hemisphere and a cone.

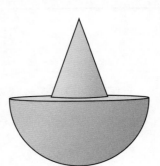

The hemisphere has a diameter of 14 cm.
The height of the cone is $2\sqrt{35}$ cm and the radius of its base is 2 cm.

Work out the total volume of the spinning top.
Give your answer to 3 significant figures.

.... cm³

[Total 5 marks]

5 The diagram below shows a clay bowl in the shape of a hollow hemisphere.
The radius of the inside surface is 8 cm. The radius of the outside surface is 9 cm.

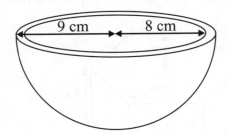

What volume of clay is needed to make the bowl?
Give your answer to 3 significant figures.

.... cm³

[Total 4 marks]

6 A silo is constructed to store grain. It is in the shape of a cone with a smaller cone removed.
The diameter of the base of the silo is 30 m and the diameter of the top of the silo is 25 m.
The height of the silo is 50 m and the height of the removed cone is 250 m.

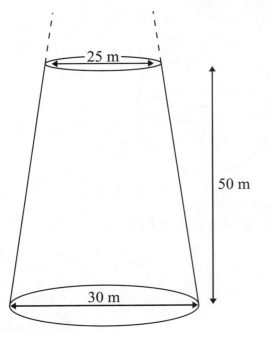

Find the volume of the silo.
Give your answer to 3 significant figures.

.... m³

[Total 5 marks]

Score:

24

Section Three — Geometric Skills

Pythagoras' Theorem

1 A ladder is 3.5 m long. For safety, when the ladder is leant against a wall, the base should never be less than 2.1 m away from the wall.

What is the maximum vertical height that the top of the ladder can safely reach to?

.... m

[Total 2 marks]

2 A triangle has a base of 10 cm. Its other two sides are both 13 cm long.

Calculate the area of the triangle.

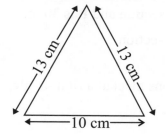

.... cm²

[Total 3 marks]

3 The diagram shows a kite *ABCD*. *AB* is 28.3 cm long. *BC* is 54.3 cm long. *BE* is 20 cm in length.

Work out the perimeter of triangle *ABC*. Give your answer to 1 decimal place.

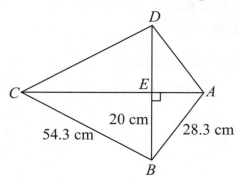

.... cm

[Total 4 marks]

4   Point *A* has coordinates (2, –1). Point *B* has coordinates (8, 8).
     Find the exact length of the line segment *AB*. Simplify your answer as much as possible.

....

[Total 3 marks]

5   A crane is made from a fixed vertical section and a pivoting section, as shown below.
     The two parts meet at the point **P**. The movable section pivots about **P**.

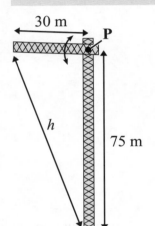

The distance between the base of the vertical section and **P** is 75 m.
The distance between the end of the pivoting section and **P** is 30 m.

The distance between the base of the vertical section
and the end of the pivoting section is *h*.

If *h* = 85 m, determine whether the two sections meet at a right-angle.
Justify your answer.

[Total 3 marks]

6   The diagram below shows a design for a badge. It is in the shape of
     part of a circle. The circle has a radius of 3.5 cm, and the length of
     the chords that form the top and bottom edges are 6 cm each.

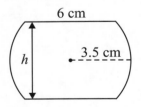

Find *h*, the height of the badge to 3 significant figures.

.... cm

[Total 4 marks]

7 The diagram below shows a cuboid, relative to the coordinate axes.

The point O is the origin $(0, 0, 0)$. The coordinates of A are $(6, 0, 0)$, of B are $(0, 3, 0)$ and of C are $(0, 0, 4)$.

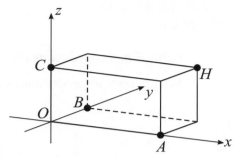

Calculate the length of the diagonal OH.
Give your answer to 3 significant figures.

$OH^2 = $ ....² + ...² + ...²

$OH = \sqrt{\rule{3cm}{0pt}}$

$OH = $ ....

....
[Total 3 marks]

8 A snow globe is made from part of a sphere, as shown below.

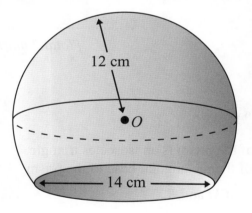

The radius of the sphere is 12 cm.
The diameter of the circular base of the snow globe is 14 cm.

Calculate the height of the snow globe.
Give your answer to 3 significant figures.

.... cm
[Total 4 marks]

Exam Practice Tip

You shouldn't be too surprised to find Pythagoras questions needing you to use your reasoning skills, often to do with circles. The hardest part is working out where the right-angled triangle actually is. One side of the triangle will usually be the radius of the circle — but possibly not where the diagram has drawn it.

Score

26

Section Three — Geometric Skills

3D Coordinates

1 A sphere is drawn relative to the coordinate axes.
The centre of the sphere is at the origin O.

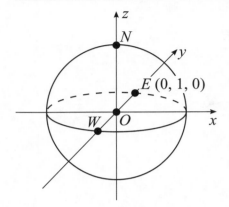

Point E has coordinates $(0, 1, 0)$.

Write down the coordinates of point N and point W.

N ....

W ....

[Total 2 marks]

2 The diagram below shows a cube placed on top of a cuboid, relative to the coordinate axes.

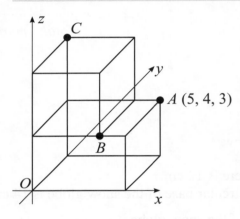

A is the point $(5, 4, 3)$
Determine the coordinates of B and C.

B ....

C ....

[Total 2 marks]

3 The diagram below shows a prism, relative to the coordinate axes.

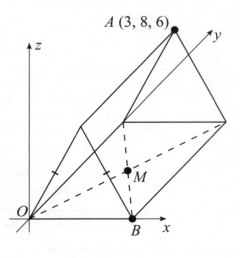

The cross-section of the prism is an isosceles triangle.
M is the midpoint of the rectangular base of the prism.

State the coordinate of M and B.

M ....

B ....

[Total 2 marks]

Score:

6

Section Three – Geometric Skills

Vectors

1   **a**, **b** and **c** are column vectors, where $\mathbf{a} = \begin{pmatrix} -3 \\ 5 \end{pmatrix}$, $\mathbf{b} = \begin{pmatrix} 5 \\ 4 \end{pmatrix}$ and $\mathbf{c} = \begin{pmatrix} -4 \\ -6 \end{pmatrix}$.

Calculate:

a)   **a** − **b**

....
[1]

b)   4**b** − **c**

....
[2]

c) |2**a** + **b** + 3**c**|

....
[4]

[Total 7 marks]

2   *ABC* is a triangle where $\overrightarrow{AB}$ = 4**a** and $\overrightarrow{BC}$ = 3**b**.

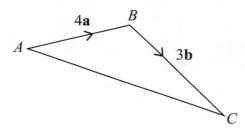

Write $\overrightarrow{AC}$ in terms of **a** and **b**.

....
[Total 1 mark]

3   In the diagram, $\overrightarrow{OA}$ = 2**a** and $\overrightarrow{OB}$ = **b**.
M is the midpoint of *AB*.

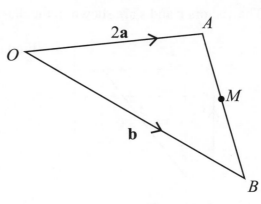

Find $\overrightarrow{OM}$ in terms of **a** and **b**.

$$\overrightarrow{OM} = \underline{\quad\quad} + \underline{\quad\quad} = \underline{\quad\quad} + \frac{1}{2}\underline{\quad\quad}$$

$$\overrightarrow{AB} = \underline{\quad} + \underline{\quad}$$

$$\overrightarrow{OM} = \underline{\quad} + \frac{1}{2}(\underline{\quad\quad}) = \underline{\quad\quad\quad}$$

....
[Total 2 marks]

4   *ABCD* is a parallelogram. $\overrightarrow{AB} = \begin{pmatrix} 4 \\ -1 \end{pmatrix}$, $\overrightarrow{AD} = \begin{pmatrix} 7 \\ 2 \end{pmatrix}$.

Draw a diagram if it helps.

Find the magnitude of $\overrightarrow{BD}$ to two decimal places.

....

[Total 3 marks]

5   *ABCD* is a parallelogram. $\overrightarrow{AB} = 2\mathbf{a}$ and $\overrightarrow{AD} = 2\mathbf{d}$.
L is the midpoint of *AC*.

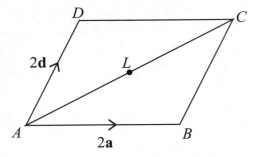

Write in terms of **a** and **d**:

a) $\overrightarrow{CD}$

....
[1]

b) $\overrightarrow{AC}$

....
[1]

c) $\overrightarrow{BL}$

....
[1]

[Total 3 marks]

6   Calculate the exact value of |**u**|, the magnitude of the vector $\mathbf{u} = \begin{pmatrix} 5 \\ -2 \\ -4 \end{pmatrix}$.

Simplify your answer as far as possible.

....

[Total 2 marks]

7   The vectors **r** and **s** are shown in the diagram below.

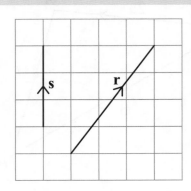

Find the magnitude of the resultant vector **r** + **s**.

....

[Total 4 marks]

Score:
22

Trigonometric Graphs

1   The diagram below shows part of the graph of $y = p + \cos qx°$.

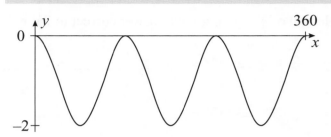

Write down the values of p and q.

$p =$ ...., $\quad q =$ ....

[Total 2 marks]

2   The function f(x) is defined by f(x) $= 4 \sin (x - 90)°$.

a)   Write down the value of the phase angle.

....................°

[1]

b)   Sketch the graph of $y =$ f(x) in the range $-360 \leq x \leq 360$.

[3]

c)   Hence, or otherwise, express f(x) in the form $a \cos x$,
where the value of a is to be determined.

f(x) = ...

[1]

[Total 5 marks]

3   f(x) $= \tan x°$ is transformed to g(x) by a multiple angle of 5.

a)   Write down the transformed function g(x).

g(x) = ...

[1]

b)   For what values of x is g(x) undefined in the range $0 \leq x \leq 90$?

....

[3]

[Total 4 marks]

Exam Practice Tip

Transformations in the y-direction act as you'd expect — positive translations move the graph right and larger magnitude scale factors make the amplitude bigger. But transformations in the x-direction are sneakier — (x + c) translates the graph left and the graph gets squashed as the scale factor increases in magnitude.

Score

11

Trigonometry — Sin, Cos, Tan

1   *X*, *Y* and *Z* are points on a circle, where *XY* is a diameter of the circle.

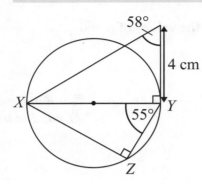

Calculate the length of *YZ*, giving your answer correct to 2 d.p.

.... 58° = $\dfrac{XY}{..............}$ ⟹ XY = ... = ... cm

.... 55° = $\dfrac{..............}{..............}$ ⟹ YZ = ...

.... cm

[Total 4 marks]

2   The diagram shows a kite *EFGH*.
Diagonal *EG* bisects the diagonal *HF* at *M*.
EM = 5 cm, *MG* = 9 cm and *HF* = 12 cm.

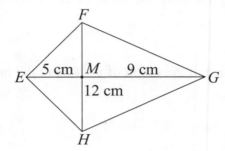

a)   Calculate the size of angle *FGM*.
Give your answer to 1 decimal place.

..........................°

[2]

b)   Calculate the size of angle *FEH*.
Give your answer to 1 decimal place.

..........................°

[3]

[Total 5 marks]

3   A regular hexagon is drawn such that all of its vertices are on the
circumference of a circle of radius 8.5 cm, as shown below.

Calculate the distance from the centre of the circle to the centre of one edge of the hexagon.
Give your answer to 2 decimal places.

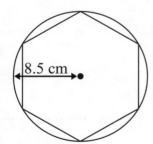

The sum of interior angles in a polygon
= (number of sides − 2) × 180°.

.... cm

[Total 4 marks]

Exam Practice Tip

In an exam, it'll help if you start by labelling the sides of a right-angled triangle, opposite (O), adjacent (A)
and hypotenuse (H) — these are easy to get muddled up. If you're working out an angle, make sure you
check whether it's sensible — if you get an angle of 720° or 0.0072°, it's probably wrong so try again.

Score

13

Related Angles

1 Write the following values in ascending order.

$$\cos(-70)° \qquad \cos 20° \qquad \cos 200° \qquad \cos 360°$$

...................., ..., ..., ...

[Total 1 mark]

2 The graph of $y = \cos x°$ is shown below for $0 \leq x \leq 360$.

As shown on the graph, $\cos 130° = -0.643$.

Give another value of x, found on this graph, where $\cos x° = -0.643$.

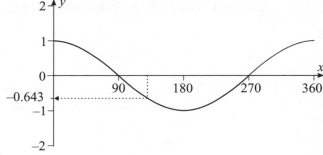

$x = $ ....

[Total 1 mark]

3 You are given that $\sin 60° = \dfrac{\sqrt{3}}{2}$. Which of the following values of x also gives $\sin x = \dfrac{\sqrt{3}}{2}$?

$$-60° \qquad 120° \qquad 240° \qquad 300°$$

....

[Total 1 mark]

4 The diagram shows a sketch of $y = \tan x°$ for $0 \leq x \leq 360$.

You are given that $\tan 18° = 0.325$.

Write down the two values of x such that $\tan x° = -0.325$ for $0 \leq x \leq 360$.

$x = $ .... and $x = $ ....

[Total 2 marks]

Score:

5

Solving Trig Equations

1   Solve $\cos x = 0.65$ for $0° \leq x \leq 360°$. Give each solution to 1 decimal place.

....

[Total 2 marks]

2   Solve the equation $5 \sin x + 2 = 0$ for $0° \leq x \leq 360°$.
Give your solutions to 1 decimal place.

....

[Total 3 marks]

3   Parts of the graphs of $y = -\sin x° + 2$ and $y = \dfrac{3}{2}$ are shown below.

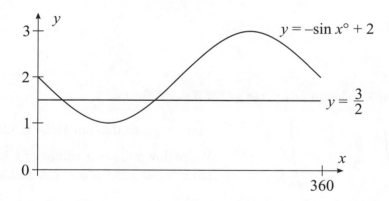

Determine the x-coordinates of the points where the graphs intersect in the range shown.

....

[Total 4 marks]

4 An athlete runs anticlockwise around a circular track, starting at *S*. Beside the track is a straight sand pit. As the athlete runs around the track, his distance, *d* metres, from the pit is $d = 24 + 21 \sin x$, where $0° \leq x \leq 360°$ is the angle he has run through, as shown below.

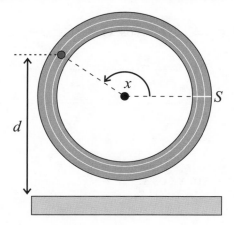

a) What is the distance, to 1 decimal place, between the athlete and the sand pit when he has run through an angle of 70°?

.... m

[1]

b) Determine the furthest distance that the athlete can be from the sand pit.

.... m

[1]

c) Calculate, to 1 decimal place, the distance that the athlete travels in one lap of the track.

.... m

[2]

d) Find the values of *x,* to the nearest degree, for which the athlete is 12 m from the sand pit.

....

[4]

[Total 8 marks]

Score:

17

Section Four — Trigonometric Skills

Trig Identities

1 Show that the equation $2(1 - \cos x) = 3 \sin^2 x$ can be written as $3 \cos^2 x - 2 \cos x - 1 = 0$.

$$2(1 - \cos x) = 3 \sin^2 x \Rightarrow 2(1 - \cos x) = 3(\text{........} - \text{......................})$$

$$\Rightarrow \text{........} - \text{.....................} = \text{........} - \text{.....................}$$

$$\Rightarrow \text{.....................} - \text{.....................} - \text{........} = O$$

[Total 2 marks]

2 Show that $\sin^2 x \tan x \equiv \tan x - \sin x \cos x$.

[Total 3 marks]

3 The function f(x) is defined by $f(x) = \dfrac{\sin^3 x}{\cos x} + \sin x \cos x$.

a) Simplify f(x).

$$f(x) = \frac{\sin^3 x}{\cos x} + \sin x \cos x \equiv \frac{\text{...............} + \text{.............................}}{\cos x}$$

$$\equiv \frac{\text{...........} (\text{....................} + \text{....................})}{\cos x}$$

$$\equiv \frac{\text{.................}}{\cos x} \equiv \text{..........................}$$

$$f(x) = \text{.....................}$$

[4]

b) Hence, solve $5f(x) = 10$ in the range $0° \leq x \leq 360°$.
Give your solutions to 1 decimal place.

....

[3]

[Total 7 marks]

Exam Practice Tip

If a trig question uses the words "simplify" or "show that", your mind should go straight to trig identities.
There are only two identities you need to know (the one with tan x and the one with sin² x and cos² x) —
so if you don't seem to be getting anywhere with one of them, maybe have a bash with the other.

Score

12

The Sine and Cosine Rules

1   In the triangle below, $AB = 12$ cm, $AC = 14$ cm and $\sin A = 0.9$.

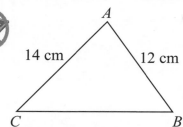

Calculate the area of the triangle.

.... cm^2

[Total 2 marks]

2   In the triangle on the right, $AB = 10$ cm, $BC = 7$ cm and angle $ABC = 85°$.

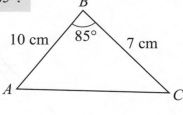

a)   Calculate the length of AC.
       Give your answer to 3 significant figures.

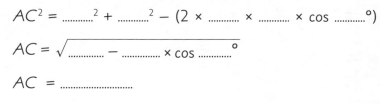

$AC^2 = \text{........}^2 + \text{........}^2 - (2 \times \text{........} \times \text{........} \times \cos \text{........}°)$

$AC = \sqrt{\text{........} - \text{........} \times \cos \text{........}°}$

$AC = \text{........................}$

.... cm

[3]

b)   Calculate the area of triangle ABC.
       Give your answer to 3 significant figures.

.... cm^2

[2]

[Total 5 marks]

3   In the triangle below, $AB = 17$ cm, $AC = 36$ cm and angle $ABC = 112°$.

Find the size of angle ACB.
Give your answer to correct to 1 d.p.

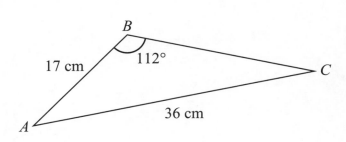

...........................°

[Total 3 marks]

4 The perimeter of triangle ABC is $(a + \sqrt{b})x$ cm.

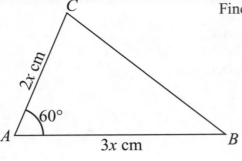

Find the values of a and b.

$a =$ .... , $b =$ ....

[Total 4 marks]

5 A castle drawbridge is supported by two chains, AB and AC. Using the information on the diagram, calculate the total length of the drawbridge, BD, correct to 3 s.f.

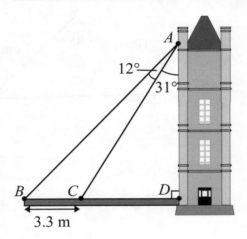

.... m

[Total 5 marks]

6 $ABCD$ is a quadrilateral.

Work out the area of $ABCD$ to 4 significant figures.
Show clearly how you get your answer.

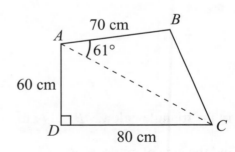

.... cm²

[Total 5 marks]

Score:

24

Section Four — Trigonometric Skills

Trigonometry with Bearings

1   An aircraft travels 225 km on a bearing of 110° from *O* to *D*.
It is then instructed to divert and travel on a bearing of 050°.
The aircraft continues on this bearing until it lands at *L*.

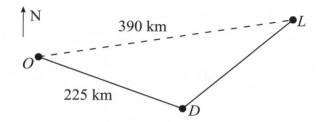

a)   The aircraft lands 390 km from its start point *O*, measured in a straight line.
Calculate the bearing on which it would have travelled to reach this point directly.

.........................°

[4]

b)   What distance did the aircraft travel from *D* to *L*?
Give your answer to 3 significant figures.

.... km

[3]

[Total 7 marks]

2   Three beacons, *X*, *Y* and *Z*, are positioned such that *X* is 50 m from *Y* and *Z* is 100 m from *Y*.
X is due north of *Y* and *Y* is on a bearing of 250° from *Z*.

Determine the distance between *X* and *Z*.
Give your answer to 3 significant figures.

.... m

[Total 4 marks]

Score

11

Comparing Data Sets

1   The numbers of fish an angler catches each day in a week are 2, 4, 1, 7, 2, 6 and 5.

Calculate the median and the semi-interquartile range of these numbers.

Start by writing the numbers in ascending order.

Median: ....   Semi-interquartile range: ....

[Total 3 marks]

2   The standard deviation of the values below is equal to $\sqrt{c}$.

$$6 \qquad 12 \qquad 10 \qquad 1 \qquad 0 \qquad 9 \qquad 4$$

Find the value of c.

$c = $ ....

[Total 3 marks]

3   Liz sells earrings. The prices in pounds of 6 pairs of earrings are given below.

$$7 \qquad 3 \qquad 5 \qquad 4 \qquad 7 \qquad 4$$

a)   Find the semi-interquartile range of the prices above.

....

[2]

b)   Calculate the standard deviation of the prices.

....

[3]

c)   Liz begins to sell a new pair of earrings costing £80.
Which of the semi-interquartile range or the standard deviation
will be least affected by this new price?
Give a reason for your answer.

....

....

[1]

[Total 6 marks]

4 The data below shows the number of strawberries collected from each plant during one harvest of strawberry patch A.

8   13   19   22   8   18   14   16   9   14   12

a) Find the median and semi-interquartile range of this data.

Median: ....   Semi-interquartile range: ....

[3]

b) Similar data was collected for the plants in strawberry patch B. The median number of strawberries collected from each plant was 10 and the semi-interquartile range was 2.

Make two valid comparisons between the plants in patch A and the plants in patch B.

....

....

....

[2]

[Total 5 marks]

5 One month, a clown performs at 8 birthday parties.
The number of children at each birthday party is given below.

22   20   16   3   15   31   22   15

a) Calculate the mean number of children at a party and the standard deviation.
Give your answers to 3 significant figures where appropriate.

Mean: ....   Standard deviation: ....

[4]

b) The following month, the mean number of children at the clown's parties was 24 and the standard deviation was 4.5.

Give two valid comments to compare the number of children at the parties for the two months.

....

....

....

[2]

[Total 6 marks]

Exam Practice Tip

Working out semi-interquartile ranges and standard deviations can be a slow process — especially when they come up on the non-calculator paper. Absolutely, definitely don't rush through it. And remember that the formula for standard deviation is given to you in the exam so there's no excuse for getting it wrong.

Score

23

Scattergraphs

1 15 pupils in a class study both Spanish and Italian.
Their end of year exam results are shown on the scattergraph below.

a) Circle the point that doesn't follow the trend.

[1]

b) Describe the strength and type of correlation
shown by the points that do follow the trend.

....

....

[1]

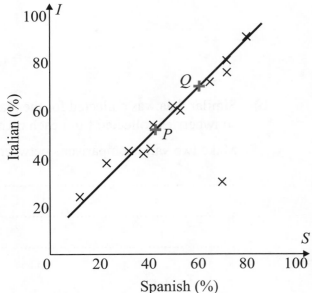

c) The points *P* and *Q* are on the line of best fit.

The point *P* corresponds to a pupil who
obtained 43% in Spanish and 52% in Italian.
The point *Q* corresponds to a pupil who
obtained 61% in Spanish and 70% in Italian.

Find the equation of the line of best fit.
Give the equation in the form $I = mS + c$.

....

[3]

d) A new pupil sits the Spanish exam, but misses the Italian exam. In Spanish, they get a result
of 37%. Use your equation to estimate the result they would have got in the Italian exam.

....................%

[1]

[Total 6 marks]

2 The manager of a shop records the number of customers who enter the shop
in the 10 days after Christmas. Her findings are shown in the scattergraph.
The manager forgets to record the number of customers on Day 3.

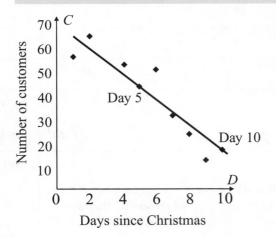

There were 44 customers on Day 5
and 19 customers on Day 10.

Work out the equation of the line of best fit and use
it to estimate the number of customers on Day 3.

....

[Total 4 marks]

Section Five — Statistical Skills

3   A furniture company is looking at how effective their advertising is.
They are comparing how much they spent on advertising in random months with
their total sales value for that month. This information is shown on the graph below.

a)   Describe the relationship between the amount
spent on advertising and the value of sales.

....

....

....

[1]

b)   Determine the equation of the line of best fit in
terms of A (advertising) and S (sales).
Give your equation in the form $aS + bA + c = 0$,
where a, b and c are integers.

Graph:
- y-axis: Sales (thousands of pounds), values 50, 100, 150, 200 with label S
- x-axis: Amount spent on advertising (thousands of pounds), values 0, 0.5, 1, 1.5, 2 with label A
- Point $X\,(0.15, 60)$
- Point $Y\,(1.85, 170)$

....

[3]

c)   Use your line of best fit to estimate, to 3 s.f., the monthly sales value
if the company spends £600 on advertising.

£ ....

[2]

d)   The company plan to increase their monthly spend on advertising to at least £3000.
They use the trend in the data above to predict future sales values.
Comment on how reliable this prediction is likely to be.

....

....

....

[2]

[Total 8 marks]

Score:

18

National 5
Mathematics

Practice Paper 1
(Non-Calculator)

Duration — 1 hour 15 minutes

Fill in these boxes and read what is printed below.

Full name of centre

Woodmill High School

Town

Dunfermline

Candidate Forename(s)

David

Candidate Surname

Agnew

Date of birth

Day		Month		Year	
2	2	0	7	0	5

Scottish candidate number

1	1	0	4	9	7	3	7	7

Total marks available for this paper — 50

You may NOT use a calculator.

Answer ALL the questions.

Write your answers in the spaces provided.

You must use **BLUE** or **BLACK** ink to write your answers.

To earn full marks you must show all of your working.

Give units with your answer where required.

You will find the formula list at the back of this book.

Total marks — 50
Attempt ALL questions

1. A straight line has equation $4 = \frac{1}{2}y + 2x$.

   Find the gradient of the line.

   2

   $8 = y + 4x$

   $= 8 + 4x$

2. Expand and simplify

   $(x - 10)(-x^2 + x + 9).$

   3

   $-x^3 + 10x^2 + x^2 + 9x - 10x - 90$

   $11x^2 - x^3 - x - 90$

3. Evaluate $\frac{3}{5}\left(\frac{5}{6} - \frac{2}{9}\right)$.

   Write your answer in its simplest form.

   2

1

MARKS

4. The diagram below shows two identical squares ABXY and YXDC.
   The squares are joined along the shared edge XY.
   The vectors **m** and **n** are represented by $\overrightarrow{AX}$ and $\overrightarrow{AY}$ respectively.

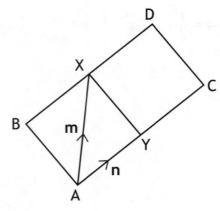

   (a) Write down $\overrightarrow{XY}$ in terms of **m** and **n**. 1

   (b) Write down $\overrightarrow{AD}$ in terms of **m** and **n**. 1

5. The function g(x) is defined by $g(x) = \sqrt{x} + \dfrac{1}{x}$.
   Express g(4) as a single fraction in its simplest form. 2

6. A farmer records the mass of his harvest over a number of years.
    The scattergraph below shows the relationship between the average
    temperature recorded on the farm, T °C, and the mass of his harvest, H kg.

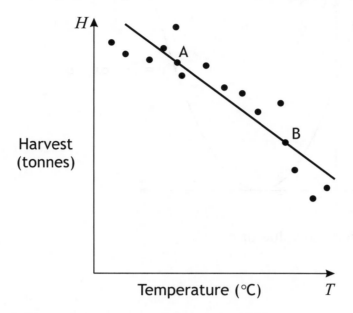

Point A represents a year with an average temperature of 10 °C
and a harvest with a mass of 77 tonnes.
Point B represents a year with an average temperature of 24 °C
and a harvest with a mass of 35 tonnes.

(a) Determine the equation of the line of best fit in terms of T and H.
    You should give your equation in its simplest form.

3

(b) Hence, estimate the mass of the harvest in a year
    with an average temperature of 20 °C.
    You should show your working.

1

3

7. The sketch below shows the parabola with equation $y = x^2 - 6x + c$.
   The minimum turning point of the parabola lies on the positive x-axis.

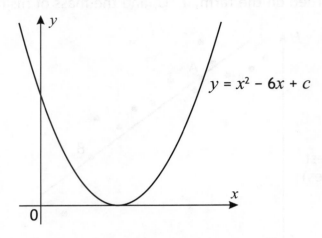

   Use the discriminant to find the value of c.

3

8. Express $\dfrac{n^5 \times \sqrt{n}}{n^{\frac{3}{2}}}$ in the form n^m, where m is an integer.

2

4

9. Make u the subject of the formula $W = \frac{1}{2}m(v^2 - u^2)$.

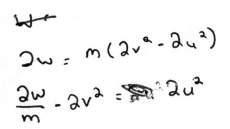

$$2w = m(2v^a - 2u^2)$$

$$\frac{2w}{m} - 2v^2 = 2u^2$$

10.

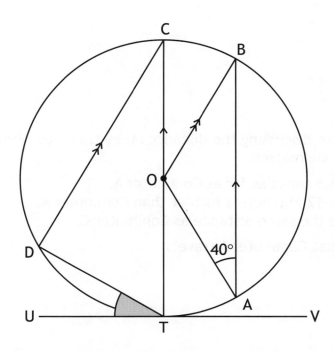

A, B, C, D and T are points on the circumference of the circle with centre O.
The line UV is a tangent to the circle, with point of contact T.
TC is parallel to AB and DC is parallel to OB.

Calculate the size of the angle DTU.

11. Show that

$$1 + \tan^2 x° \equiv \frac{1}{\cos^2 x°}.$$

2

12. Three commuters are discussing the distances they travel to work. All distances are in kilometres.

Commuter B travels 5 times as far as Commuter A.
Commuter C travels 12 kilometres further than Commuter A.
Commuter B travels the same distance as Commuter C.

Find the distance that Commuter A travels.

13. An office block has $x + 3$ floors.
On each floor, there are $x + 12$ workstations.

   (a) Write down an expression for the number of
       workstations in the office block.

1

   (b) A neighbouring office block has 112 workstations. This office block
       has 42 more workstations than the office block from part (a).

       Solve an appropriate quadratic equation to find the value of x.

4

14. Part of the graphs of $y = i \sin jx°$ and $y = \sin x° + k$ are drawn below.

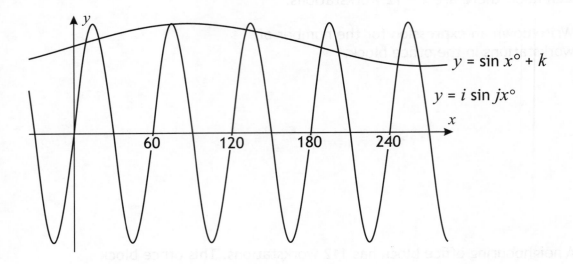

The period and amplitude of $y = i \sin jx°$ are 60 and 5 respectively.

(a) State the values of i and j.

(b) The maximum points of $y = \sin x° + k$ have the same y-coordinate as the maximum points of $y = i \sin jx°$.

State the value of k.

MARKS

2

1

8

15. The rectangles OABC and OPQR, shown below, are mathematically similar.

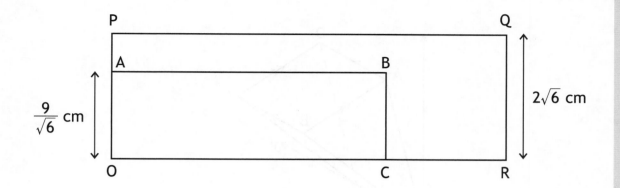

The length of OA is $\dfrac{9}{\sqrt{6}}$ cm and the length of QR is $2\sqrt{6}$ cm.

The area of rectangle OPQR is 160 cm².
Calculate the area of the six-sided shape PQRCBA.

4

16. A triangular prism is shown below, relative to the coordinate axes.
Point O is the origin (0, 0, 0).

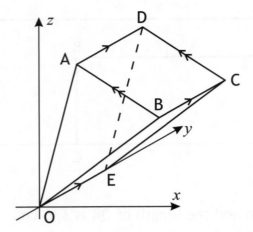

The face ABCD is a square.
The line OE lies on the y-axis.
Point A has coordinates (2, 0, 8) and point B has coordinates (6, 0, 5).

(a) Find the coordinates of point C.   3

(b) Determine whether the triangular face OAB is right-angled.
Fully justify your answer.   4

10

National 5
Mathematics
Practice Paper 2

Duration — 1 hour 50 minutes

Fill in these boxes and read what is printed below.

Full name of centre

Town

Forename(s)

Surname

Date of birth

Day	Month	Year

Scottish candidate number

Total marks available for this paper — 60

You may use a calculator.

Answer ALL the questions.

Write your answers in the spaces provided.

You must use **BLUE** or **BLACK** ink to write your answers.

To earn full marks you must show all of your working.

Give units with your answer where required.

You will find the formula list at the back of this book.

Total marks — 60
Attempt ALL questions

1. A straight line is shown on the diagram below.
   U and V are points on the line.

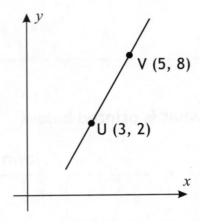

   Find the equation of the line in the form $y = mx + c$.

   3

   $\dfrac{8-2}{5-3}$ $\dfrac{6}{3} = 2$ $(3, 2)$
                                    $a \quad b$

   $y = 2x + c$

   $y - b = m(x - a)$ $y = 2x - 4$

   $y - 2 = 2(x - 3)$

   $y - 2 = 2x - 6$

2. Solve this inequality algebraically

   $7 + 3(x - 2) < x - 11$.

   3

   $7 + 3x - 6 < x - 11$

   $7 + 3x < x - 5$

   $7 + 2x < -5$

   $2x < -12$

   $x < -6$

1

3. Fully factorise

$7t^2 - 63.$

$7(t+3)(t-3)$

4. The triangle shown below has an area of 18 cm².

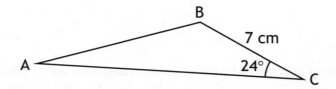

Calculate the length of the side AC.
Give your answer to three significant figures.

$\frac{24}{360}$

Area = $\frac{1}{2}$ AB sin C

$18 = \frac{1}{2}$ AB sin C

5. A delivery company wants to increase the number of daily deliveries it makes.
It increases the number of deliveries by 5% each month for 6 months.

(a) Given that the number of daily deliveries made was originally 33,
calculate the number of daily deliveries made after 6 months.
Give your answer to the nearest whole number.

3

$$33 \times 1.05^6$$

$$= \underline{44.2}$$

$$= \underline{44}$$

(b) Another delivery company has increased the number of daily deliveries
that they make by 15%. They now make 46 daily deliveries.

How many daily deliveries did they previously make?

3

$$46 \times 0.85$$

3

6. During the daytime, a train makes the return trip between the city and the beach 6 times.
On the same day, the train makes the return trip between the city and the lake 7 times.

In total, the train takes 201 minutes to make all these journeys.

(a) Show this information in an equation.

$$6b + 7l = 201$$

1

(b) During the night-time, the train makes the return trip between the city and the beach twice and between the city and the lake 3 times. In total, the train takes 75 minutes to make these journeys.
Show this information in an equation.

$$2b + 3l = 75$$

1

(c) Determine how many minutes it takes the train to make one return trip between the city and the beach and how many minutes it takes the train to make one return trip between the city and the lake.

$$6b + 7l = 201$$
$$2b + 3l = 75$$

$$6b + 9l = \cancel{75}\ 225$$

$$2l = 24$$
$$\underline{l = 12}$$

$$2b + 3(12) = 75$$
$$2b + 36 = 75$$
$$2b = 39$$
$$\underline{b = 19.5}$$

4

4

7. A grain of sand has a mass, on average, of 6.7×10^{-4} g.
A section of beach is excavated and the total mass of sand collected is 134 kg.

Use this information to estimate the number of grains of sand collected.
Give your answer in scientific notation.

2

$0.0067\ g$

$$\frac{134,000}{0.0067}$$

$= 20\,000\,000$

8. A helicopter follows the path given by the vector $\mathbf{h} = \begin{pmatrix} 55 \\ 20 \\ -1 \end{pmatrix}$.

Find $|\mathbf{h}|$, the magnitude of $\mathbf{h}$. Give your answer to three significant figures.

2

9. Express

$$\frac{20p^2 - 5p}{q^2} \div \frac{5p}{9q}, \qquad q \neq 0$$

as a single fraction in its simplest form.

3

$$\frac{20p^2 - 5p}{q^2} \times \frac{9q}{5p}$$

$$\frac{(20p^2 - 5p)(9q)}{(q^2)(5p)}$$

$$\frac{180pq^2 - 45pq}{5pq^2}$$

$$\frac{36pq^2 - 9pq}{pq^2}$$

$$\frac{36p - 9}{q}$$

10. Solve the equation $3 - 12 \sin x° = 7$ in the range $0 \leq x \leq 360$.

3

$$3 - 12 \sin = 7$$

$$12 \sin = \frac{-4}{}$$

$$\sin = \frac{-4}{12}$$

$$\sin = 19.471$$

6

11. A band is performing in 10 different locations.
The ticket sales for each performance are shown below:

558   349   394   264   258   589   782   367   745   398

(a) Calculate the median and semi-interquartile range of the data.

3

(b) A solo artist also performs on a number of occasions. The median of her ticket sales was 567 and the semi-interquartile range was 234.

Make two valid comparisons between the ticket sales of the band and those of the solo artist.

2

7

12. A mobile phone network builds three new masts.

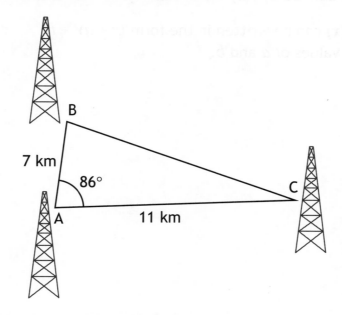

The distance between masts A and B is 7 km.
The distance between masts A and C is 11 km.
The angle between AB and AC is 86°.

Calculate the distance between masts B and C.

3

8

13. The function $f(x)$ is defined by $f(x) = x^2 + 14x - 3$.

(a) The function $f(x)$ can be written in the form $(x + a)^2 + b$.
Determine the values of a and b.

2

(b) Sketch the graph of $y = f(x)$.
You should clearly indicate the coordinates of the point at which the graph
intersects the y-axis and the coordinates of the turning point of the graph.

3

9

14. A circle has a diameter of 12 cm.
A sector is removed from the circle. The sector has an area of 25 cm².

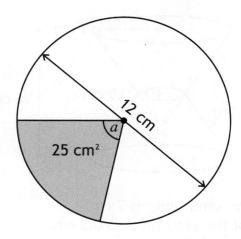

12 cm

a

25 cm²

Calculate *a*, the size of the angle of the sector.

3

MARKS

15. A sand timer is in the shape of two identical cones, each with smaller identical cones removed. This is shown in the diagram below.

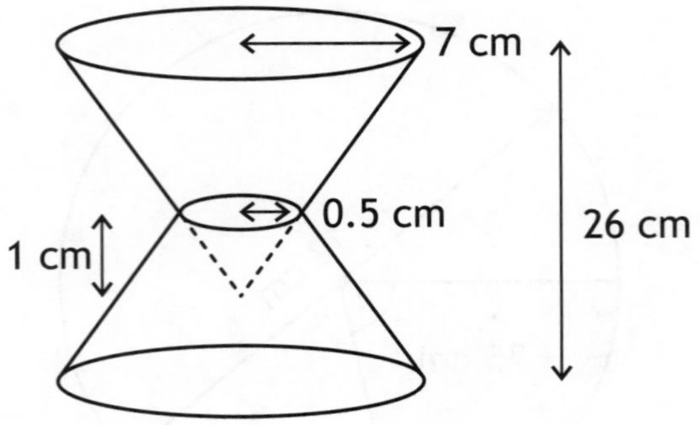

The radius of the top of the sand timer is 7 cm.
The radius of the centre of the sand timer is 0.5 cm.
The height of a removed cone is 1 cm.
The total height of the sand timer is 26 cm.

Calculate the volume of the sand timer.
Give your answer correct to 2 significant figures. **5**

16. A lifeboat station is located at the point O. A transmitter is attached to a buoy at the point T, 13 km south of O. A boat in distress is located at the point D, 3 km east of the buoy.

North

O

13 km

T

3 km

D

(a) Calculate the exact distance between O and D.

2

(b) A lifeboat is on patrol at point L, 15 km from the lifeboat station on a bearing of 097°.

Use this information and the information in part (a) to calculate the distance between the lifeboat on patrol and the boat in distress.

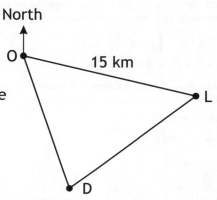

North

O

15 km

L

D

4

Answers

Section One — Numerical Skills

Page 5: Fractions

1 $4\frac{2}{5} + 3\frac{1}{4} = \frac{22}{5} + \frac{13}{4} = \frac{88}{20} + \frac{65}{20} = \frac{88+65}{20} = \frac{153}{20}$ or $7\frac{13}{20}$
  [2 marks available — 1 mark for a correct method for adding fractions, 1 mark for the correct answer in its simplest form]

2 $2\frac{5}{6} - 1\frac{1}{5} = \frac{17}{6} - \frac{6}{5} = \frac{85}{30} - \frac{36}{30} = \frac{85-36}{30} = \frac{49}{30}$ or $1\frac{19}{30}$
  [2 marks available — 1 mark for a correct method for subtracting fractions, 1 mark for the correct answer in its simplest form]

3 $4\frac{3}{5} \times 2\frac{1}{3} = \frac{23}{5} \times \frac{7}{3} = \frac{23 \times 7}{5 \times 3} = \frac{161}{15}$ or $10\frac{11}{15}$
  [2 marks available — 1 mark for a correct method for multiplying fractions, 1 mark for the correct answer in its simplest form]

4 $4\frac{1}{3} \div 2\frac{3}{5} = \frac{13}{3} \div \frac{13}{5} = \frac{13}{3} \times \frac{5}{13} = \frac{1}{3} \times \frac{5}{1} = \frac{5}{3}$ or $1\frac{2}{3}$
  [2 marks available — 1 mark for a correct method for dividing fractions, 1 mark for the correct answer in its simplest form]

5 $\frac{3}{8}\left(1\frac{2}{5} - \frac{4}{3}\right) = \frac{3}{8}\left(\frac{7}{5} - \frac{4}{3}\right) = \frac{3}{8}\left(\frac{21}{15} - \frac{20}{15}\right)$
   $= \frac{3}{8} \times \frac{1}{15} = \frac{1}{8} \times \frac{1}{5} = \frac{1}{40}$
  [2 marks available — 1 mark for correct working, 1 mark for the correct answer in its simplest form]

6 First work out the multiplication:
   $2\frac{1}{4} \times 2\frac{1}{3} = \frac{9}{4} \times \frac{7}{3} = \frac{63}{12} = \frac{21}{4}$

   Then do the subtraction:
   $7\frac{1}{5} - \frac{21}{4} = \frac{36}{5} - \frac{21}{4} = \frac{144}{20} - \frac{105}{20} = \frac{39}{20}$ or $1\frac{19}{20}$
  [3 marks available — 1 mark for the correct method for multiplication, 1 mark for the correct method for subtraction, 1 mark for the correct answer in its simplest form]

Pages 6-8: Percentages

1 20% increase = 1 + 0.2 = 1.2, £927 × 1.2 = £1112.40
  [2 marks available — 1 mark for a correct method, 1 mark for the correct answer]
  Instead of finding the multiplier (1.2), you could have found 20% by multiplying by 0.2, then added this onto the original amount. You need to write your answer as it is here though — because you're working with money, writing 1112.4 like your calculator shows wouldn't be quite right.

2 At the end of 2014 there were 5000 × 1.12 = 5600 pine trees in the forest. At the end of 2015, there were 5600 × 1.08 = 6048 pine trees in the forest.
  [3 marks available — 1 mark for a correct method to increase the number of trees, 1 mark for finding the number of trees at the end of 2014, 1 mark for finding the number of trees at the end of 2015]

3 54 000 = 90%
   54 000 ÷ 90 = 600 = 1%
   600 × 100 = 100% = 60 000 seats
  [3 marks available — 1 mark for showing that 54 000 is 90%, 1 mark for a correct method to find 100%, 1 mark for the correct answer]

4 £15 714 = 108%
   £15 714 ÷ 108 = £145.50 = 1%
   £145.50 × 100 = 100% = £14 550
  [3 marks available — 1 mark for showing that £15 714 is 108%, 1 mark for a correct method to find 100%, 1 mark for the correct answer]

5 135 cm = 112.5%
   135 cm ÷ 112.5 = 1.2 cm = 1%
   1.2 cm × 100 = 100% = 120 cm
  [3 marks available — 1 mark for showing that 135 cm is 112.5%, 1 mark for a correct method to find 100%, 1 mark for the correct answer]

6 £11 549 = 70%
   £11 549 ÷ 70 = £164.9857... = 1%
   £164.9857... × 100 = 100% = £16 498.57...
   $\qquad\qquad\qquad$ = £16 499 to the nearest £
  [3 marks available — 1 mark for showing that £11 549 is 70%, 1 mark for a correct method to find 100%, 1 mark for the correct answer to the required level of accuracy]

7 Population after 15 years = $2000 \times (1 - 0.08)^{15}$
   $\qquad\qquad\qquad\qquad = 2000 \times (0.92)^{15}$
   $\qquad\qquad\qquad\qquad = 572.59... = 573$ fish.
  [3 marks available — 1 mark for the correct multiplier, 1 mark for raising to the correct power, 1 mark for the correct answer]

8 In 3 years she will owe:
   $£750 \times (1 + 0.06)^3 = £750 \times (1.06)^3 = £893.262$
   $\qquad\qquad\qquad\qquad\quad = £893.26$ (to the nearest penny)
  [3 marks available — 1 mark for the correct multiplier, 1 mark for raising to the correct power, 1 mark for the correct answer]

9 After 4 years, Mrs Khan will have:
   $£2500 \times (1.045)^4 = £2981.296... = £2981.30$ (to the nearest penny)
  [3 marks available — 1 mark for the correct multiplier, 1 mark for raising to the correct power, 1 mark for the correct answer]

10 In 5 years, the house will be worth:
   $£135\,000 \times (1.15)^5 = £271\,533.22... = £272\,000$ (3 s.f.)
  [3 marks available — 1 mark for the correct multiplier, 1 mark for raising to the correct power, 1 mark for the correct answer]

11 Half the original value is £15 000 ÷ 2 = £7500
   After n years, the car is worth $15\,000 \times 0.89^n$
   Use trial and error to find the value of n:
   After 5 years, the car is worth $15\,000 \times 0.89^5 = £8376.09$ (2 d.p.)
   After 6 years, the car is worth $15\,000 \times 0.89^6 = £7454.72$ (2 d.p.)
   So the car will be worth less than half its original value after 6 years.
  [3 marks available — 1 mark for the correct multiplier, 1 mark for a correct method for finding the value of the car after n years, 1 mark for the correct answer]
  5 years was a lucky guess — don't worry if it takes a couple of guesses to get close to the value you're looking for.

Page 9: The Laws of Indices

1 $5^{-2} = \frac{1}{5^2} = \frac{1}{25}$ *[1 mark]*

2 $16^{\frac{3}{4}} = \left(16^{\frac{1}{4}}\right)^3 = (2)^3 = 8$
  [2 marks available — 1 mark for interpreting the index correctly, 1 mark for the correct final answer]

3 $y^{-3} = \frac{1}{y^3}$, $y^1 = y$, $y^0 = 1$, $y^{\frac{1}{3}} = \sqrt[3]{y}$,
   so the correct order is: $y^{-3} \quad y^0 \quad y^{\frac{1}{3}} \quad y^1 \quad y^3$
  [2 marks available — 2 marks for all 5 in the correct order, otherwise 1 mark for any 4 in the correct relative order]
  If you can't identify which expression is the smallest just by looking at them, try substituting a value for y into all the expressions and working out the answer. Then it'll be easy to tell which is the smallest.

4 $\frac{5x^3}{\sqrt{x}} = \frac{5x^3}{x^{\frac{1}{2}}} = 5x^3 \times x^{-\frac{1}{2}} = 5x^{\frac{5}{2}}$
  [2 marks available — 1 mark for writing the denominator as a power of x, 1 mark for the correct final answer]

5 $5a^{\frac{3}{2}} \times (2a^{\frac{5}{2}})^3 = (5 \times 2^3) \times (a^{\frac{3}{2}} \times a^{\frac{15}{2}}) = 40a^{\frac{3+15}{2}} = 40a^9$

[3 marks available — 1 mark for simplifying $(2a^{\frac{5}{2}})^3$, 1 mark for multiplying constant terms, 1 mark for adding powers of a to give correct answer]

6 $\dfrac{12n^{13}}{2n \times 3n^4} = \dfrac{12n^{13}}{6n^5} = 2n^8$

[3 marks available — 1 mark for simplifying the denominator, 1 mark for cancelling constant terms, 1 mark for simplifying powers to give correct answer]

Pages 10-11: Scientific Notation

1 time (s) = distance (miles) ÷ speed (miles/s)
= $(9.3 \times 10^7) \div (1.86 \times 10^5)$ seconds = 5×10^2 seconds

[2 marks available — 1 mark for a correct method, 1 mark for the correct answer, given in scientific notation]

2 $(4.5 \times 10^9) \div (1.5 \times 10^8) = (4.5 \div 1.5) \times (10^9 \div 10^8)$
$= 3 \times 10^1 = 30$

So the distance from Neptune to the Sun is 30 times greater than the distance from the Earth to the Sun.

[3 marks available — 1 mark for dividing, 1 mark for a correct method for dividing, 1 mark for the correct answer]

3 2 hours = 120 minutes, so the number of revolutions is:
$(1.2 \times 10^4) \times 120 = 1\,440\,000 = 1.44 \times 10^6$

[2 marks available — 1 mark for a correct method, 1 mark for the correct answer, given in scientific notation]

4 In 150 g of sugar, there are
$150 \div (2 \times 10^{-4}) = (1.5 \times 10^2) \div (2 \times 10^{-4})$
$= (1.5 \div 2) \times (10^2 \div 10^{-4})$
$= 0.75 \times 10^6 = 7.5 \times 10^5$ grains of sugar

[3 marks available — 1 mark for dividing, 1 mark for a correct method for dividing, 1 mark for the correct answer]

5 a) number of tablets = dose (grams) ÷ dose per tablet (grams)
$= (4 \times 10^{-4}) \div (8 \times 10^{-5}) = (4 \div 8) \times (10^{-4} \div 10^{-5})$
$= 0.5 \times 10^1 = 5$

[3 marks available — 1 mark for dividing, 1 mark for a correct method for dividing, 1 mark for the correct answer]

b) new dose = 4×10^{-4} grams + 6×10^{-5} grams
$= 4 \times 10^{-4}$ grams + 0.6×10^{-4} grams
$= (4 + 0.6) \times 10^{-4}$ grams = 4.6×10^{-4} grams per day

[3 marks available — 1 mark for adding, 1 mark for a correct method for adding, 1 mark for the correct answer given in scientific notation]

You could have done this one by turning 4×10^{-4} into 40×10^{-5} and adding it to 6×10^{-5} instead.

6 Volume of cylindrical pipeline
= area of circular cross-section × length = $\pi r^2 \times l$
$= \pi \times (1.06 \div 2)^2 \times (1.05 \times 10^6)$
$= 926\,597.045... = 9.265... \times 10^5 = 9.3 \times 10^5$ m³ (2 s.f.)

[3 marks available — 1 mark for substituting into the volume formula correctly, 1 mark for finding the volume, 1 mark for the correct answer given in scientific notation to the required level of accuracy]

7 Total mass of ship and passengers = $7.59 \times 10^7 + 2.1 \times 10^5$
$= 76\,110\,000 = 7.611 \times 10^7$ kg
$(2.1 \times 10^5) \div (7.611 \times 10^7) = 0.002759...$
$0.002759... \times 100 = 0.28$ % (2 s.f.)

[3 marks available — 1 mark for finding the correct total mass, 1 mark for a correct method for finding the percentage, 1 mark for the correct answer to the required level of accuracy]

Page 12: Manipulating Surds

1 $2\sqrt{50} = 2\sqrt{25 \times 2} = 2 \times 5\sqrt{2} = 10\sqrt{2}$
$(\sqrt{2})^3 = \sqrt{2} \times \sqrt{2} \times \sqrt{2} = (\sqrt{2})^2 \times \sqrt{2} = 2\sqrt{2}$
So $2\sqrt{50} - (\sqrt{2})^3 = 10\sqrt{2} - 2\sqrt{2} = 8\sqrt{2}$

[3 marks available — 1 mark for correctly simplifying $2\sqrt{50}$, 1 mark for correctly simplifying $(\sqrt{2})^3$, 1 mark for the correct answer]

2 $\dfrac{6}{\sqrt{20}} = \dfrac{6\sqrt{20}}{20} = \dfrac{6\sqrt{4 \times 5}}{20} = \dfrac{6 \times \sqrt{4} \times \sqrt{5}}{20} = \dfrac{12\sqrt{5}}{20} = \dfrac{3\sqrt{5}}{5}$

[3 marks available — 1 mark for rationalising the denominator, 1 mark for simplifying the surd, 1 mark for the correct final answer in its simplest form]

3 $\sqrt{99} = \sqrt{9 \times 11} = 3\sqrt{11}$ *[1 mark]*

$\dfrac{22}{\sqrt{11}} = \dfrac{22\sqrt{11}}{11} = 2\sqrt{11}$ *[1 mark]*

So $\sqrt{99} + \dfrac{22}{\sqrt{11}} = 3\sqrt{11} + 2\sqrt{11} = 5\sqrt{11}$ *[1 mark]*

[3 marks available in total — as above]

4 $\dfrac{6 + \sqrt{8}}{\sqrt{2}} = \dfrac{\sqrt{2}(6 + \sqrt{8})}{2} = \dfrac{6\sqrt{2} + \sqrt{16}}{2} = \dfrac{6\sqrt{2} + 4}{2} = 3\sqrt{2} + 2$

[4 marks available — 1 mark for multiplying numerator and denominator by $\sqrt{2}$, 1 mark for multiplying out brackets on numerator, 1 mark for simplifying $\sqrt{16}$, 1 mark for cancelling to obtain correct answer]

Section Two — Algebraic Skills

Pages 13-14: Expanding Brackets

1 $5a(3a + 6ab) = (5a \times 3a) + (5a \times 6ab) = 15a^2 + 30a^2b$ *[1 mark]*

2 $3p(8 - p) - 4p(2p - 7)$
$= [(3p \times 8) + (3p \times -p)] - [(4p \times 2p) + (4p \times -7)]$
$= 24p - 3p^2 - 8p^2 + 28p$ *[1 mark]* $= 52p - 11p^2$ *[1 mark]*
[2 marks available in total — as above]

3 $4a^2(2a - 5) + a(3a + 4a^2)$
$= [(4a^2 \times 2a) + (4a^2 \times -5)] + [(a \times 3a) + (a \times 4a^2)]$
$= 8a^3 - 20a^2 + 3a^2 + 4a^3$ *[1 mark]* $= 12a^3 - 17a^2$ *[1 mark]*
[2 marks available in total — as above]

4 $(4t - 3)(2t + 5) = (4t \times 2t) + (4t \times 5) + (-3 \times 2t) + (-3 \times 5)$
$= 8t^2 + 20t - 6t - 15$ *[1 mark]* $= 8t^2 + 14t - 15$ *[1 mark]*
[2 marks available in total — as above]

5 $(2x + 9)^2 = (2x + 9)(2x + 9)$
$= (2x \times 2x) + (2x \times 9) + (9 \times 2x) + (9 \times 9)$
$= 4x^2 + 18x + 18x + 81$ *[1 mark]* $= 4x^2 + 36x + 81$ *[1 mark]*
[2 marks available in total — as above]

6 Area = ½ × base × height
$= \frac{1}{2} \times (2x + 6) \times (x - 1) = \frac{1}{2} \times (2x + 6)(x - 1)$ *[1 mark]*
$= \frac{1}{2} \times [(2x \times x) + (2x \times -1) + (6 \times x) + (6 \times -1)]$
$= \frac{1}{2} \times (2x^2 - 2x + 6x - 6)$ *[1 mark]*
$= \frac{1}{2} \times (2x^2 + 4x - 6) = x^2 + 2x - 3$ *[1 mark]*
[3 marks available in total — as above]

You could also have multiplied (2x + 6) by ½ first of all. The area would then just be (x + 3)(x − 1), which is actually a bit simpler to multiply out.

7 $(2x + 3)(x^2 - 2x + 2)$
$= (2x \times x^2) + (2x \times -2x) + (2x \times 2) + (3 \times x^2) + (3 \times -2x) + (3 \times 2)$
$= 2x^3 - 4x^2 + 4x + 3x^2 - 6x + 6 = 2x^3 - x^2 - 2x + 6$

[3 marks available — 1 mark for three terms correct, 1 mark for the remaining three terms correct, 1 mark for a fully correct answer with like terms collected]

8 a) Area = $(x - 9)(x + 2) = (x \times x) + (x \times 2) + (-9 \times x) + (-9 \times 2)$
$= x^2 + 2x - 9x - 18$ *[1 mark]* $= x^2 - 7x - 18$ *[1 mark]*
[2 marks available in total — as above]

b) Volume = $(2x - 3)(x^2 - 7x - 18)$
$= (2x \times x^2) + (2x \times -7x) + (2x \times -18)$
$\quad + (-3 \times x^2) + (-3 \times -7x) + (-3 \times -18)$
$= 2x^3 - 14x^2 - 36x - 3x^2 + 21x + 54$
$= 2x^3 - 17x^2 - 15x + 54$

[3 marks available — 1 mark for three terms correct, 1 mark for the remaining three terms correct, 1 mark for a fully correct answer with like terms collected]

Page 15: Factorising

1   $7y - 21y^2 = 7(y - 3y^2) = 7y(1 - 3y)$ *[1 mark]*

2   $2v^3w + 8v^2w^2 = 2(v^3w + 4v^2w^2) = 2v^2w(v + 4w)$ *[1 mark]*

3   $x^2 - 16 = x^2 - 4^2 = (x + 4)(x - 4)$ *[1 mark]*

4   $9n^2 - 4m^2 = (3n)^2 - (2m)^2 = (3n + 2m)(3n - 2m)$ *[1 mark]*

5   $3y^2 - 27 = 3(y^2 - 9) = 3(y + 3)(y - 3)$
[2 marks available — 1 mark for taking out a factor of 3, 1 mark for the correct answer]

Pages 16-17: Solving Equations

1   $\frac{5}{4}(2c - 1) = 3c - 2$
$5(2c - 1) = 4(3c - 2)$ *[1 mark]*
$(5 \times 2c) + (5 \times -1) = (4 \times 3c) + (4 \times -2)$
$10c - 5 = 12c - 8$
$12c - 10c = 8 - 5$ *[1 mark]*
$2c = 3$ so $c = \frac{3}{2}$ or 1.5 *[1 mark]*
[3 marks available in total — as above]

2   $\frac{8 - 2x}{3} + \frac{2x + 4}{9} = 12$
$\frac{9(8 - 2x)}{3} + \frac{9(2x + 4)}{9} = 9 \times 12$
$3(8 - 2x) + (2x + 4) = 108$
$24 - 6x + 2x + 4 = 108$
$6x - 2x = 24 + 4 - 108$
$4x = -80$ so $x = -20$
[3 marks available — 1 mark for getting rid of the fractions, 1 mark for expanding the brackets, 1 mark for correct answer]

3   $2x + 6 = 5(x - 3)$ *[1 mark]*
$2x + 6 = 5x - 15$
$21 = 3x$ *[1 mark]*
$x = 7$ cm *[1 mark]*
So one side of the triangle measures $2(7) + 6 = 20$ cm *[1 mark]*
[4 marks available in total — as above]

4   The perimeter is $(2x - 2) + (x + 1) + (22 - x) + (3x + 2)$, so...
$(2x - 2) + (x + 1) + (22 - x) + (3x + 2) = 58$ *[1 mark]*
$2x + x - x + 3x = 58 + 2 - 1 - 22 - 2$ *[1 mark]*
$5x = 35$
$x = 7$ *[1 mark]*
[3 marks available in total — as above]

5   a) $2(5x - 8) + 2(2x + 3) = 2(3x + 6) + 2y$ *[1 mark]*
$14x - 10 = 6x + 12 + 2y$
$8x - 22 = 2y$ *[1 mark]*
$y = 4x - 11$ *[1 mark]*
[3 marks available in total — as above]

  b) $14x - 10 = 32$ *[1 mark]*
$\Rightarrow 14x = 42 \Rightarrow x = 3$ *[1 mark]*
$y = 4x - 11$ so if $x = 3$, $y = 1$ *[1 mark]*
[3 marks available in total — as above]

Page 18: Inequalities

1   a) $6q - 8 < 40$, so $6q < 48$ *[1 mark]* and $q < 8$ *[1 mark]*
[2 marks available in total — as above]

  b) $\frac{3x}{4} \leq 9$, so $3x \leq 36$ *[1 mark]* and $x \leq 12$ *[1 mark]*
[2 marks available in total — as above]

2   a) $7x - 2 < 2x - 42$, so $5x < -40$ *[1 mark]* and $x < -8$ *[1 mark]*
[2 marks available in total — as above]

  b) $9 - 4x > 17 - 2x$, so $-8 > 2x$ *[1 mark]* and $x < -4$ *[1 mark]*
[2 marks available in total — as above]

3   $4 - 2p \leq 2p + 5$, so $-1 \leq 4p$ *[1 mark]* and $-\frac{1}{4} \leq p$ *[1 mark]*
[2 marks available in total — as above]

4   $13x + 3 \geq 3(5 - x)$
$13x + 3 \geq 15 - 3x$ *[1 mark]*
$16x \geq 12$ *[1 mark]*
$x \geq \frac{3}{4}$ *[1 mark]*
[3 marks available in total — as above]

5   $-x < 9x + 2(x - 1)$
$-x < 9x + 2x - 2$ *[1 mark]*
$2 < 12x$ *[1 mark]*
$\frac{1}{6} < x$ *[1 mark]*
[3 marks available in total — as above]

Pages 19-20: Rearranging Formulas

1   $F = \frac{9}{5}C + 32$, so $\frac{9}{5}C = F - 32$ and $C = \frac{5}{9}(F - 32)$
[2 marks available — 1 mark for subtracting 32 from each side, 1 mark for the correct answer]

2   a) $P = \frac{V^2}{R}$, so $PR = V^2$ *[1 mark]*, $R = \frac{V^2}{P}$ *[1 mark]*
[2 marks available in total — as above]

  b)   From a), $PR = V^2$ so $V = \pm\sqrt{PR}$ *[1 mark]*

3   $s = \frac{1}{2}gt^2$, so $gt^2 = 2s$ *[1 mark]*, $t^2 = \frac{2s}{g}$ *[1 mark]*,
$t = \sqrt{\frac{2s}{g}}$ *[1 mark]*
[3 marks available in total — as above]

4   $a + y = \frac{b - y}{a}$, so...
$a(a + y) = b - y$ *[1 mark]*, $a^2 + ay = b - y$,
$ay + y = b - a^2$ *[1 mark]*, $y(a + 1) = b - a^2$ *[1 mark]*,
$y = \frac{b - a^2}{a + 1}$ *[1 mark]*
[4 marks available in total — as above]

5   $v = \sqrt{\frac{2GM}{R}}$, so $v^2 = \frac{2GM}{R}$ *[1 mark]*,
$Rv^2 = 2GM$ *[1 mark]*, $M = \frac{Rv^2}{2G}$ *[1 mark]*
[3 marks available in total — as above]

6   a) $\frac{v^2}{2} + gz + \frac{p}{D} = c$ so $\frac{p}{D} = c - \frac{v^2}{2} - gz$ *[1 mark]*,
$p = D\left(c - \frac{v^2}{2} - gz\right)$ *[1 mark]*
[2 marks available in total — as above]

  b) $\frac{v^2}{2} + gz + \frac{p}{D} = c$ so $\frac{v^2}{2} = c - gz - \frac{p}{D}$ *[1 mark]*,
$v^2 = 2\left(c - gz - \frac{p}{D}\right)$ *[1 mark]*,
$v = \pm\sqrt{2\left(c - gz - \frac{p}{D}\right)}$ *[1 mark]*
[3 marks available in total – as above]

7   $x = \frac{1 + n}{1 - n}$, so $x(1 - n) = 1 + n$ *[1 mark]*,
$x - xn = 1 + n$, $x - 1 = xn + n$ *[1 mark]*,
$x - 1 = n(x + 1)$ *[1 mark]*,
$n = \frac{x - 1}{1 + x}$ *[1 mark]*
[4 marks available in total — as above]

Page 21: Functions

1   $f(7.5) = \frac{3}{2(7.5) + 5} = \frac{3}{20} = 0.15$
[2 marks available — 1 mark for substituting 7.5 into the function, 1 mark for the correct answer]

2   a) $f(9) = 2 \times 9^2 + 3 = 2 \times 81 + 3 = 162 + 3 = 165$
[2 marks available — 1 mark for substituting 9 into the function, 1 mark for the correct answer]

  b) $g(21) = \sqrt{2 \times 21 - 6} = \sqrt{36} = 6$
[2 marks available — 1 mark for substituting 21 into the function, 1 mark for the correct answer]

  c) $g(a) = 0$ so $\sqrt{2a - 6} = 0$ *[1 mark]* $\Rightarrow 2a - 6 = 0$ *[1 mark]*
$\Rightarrow 2a = 6 \Rightarrow a = 3$ *[1 mark]*
[3 marks available in total — as above]

3   $h(11) = \frac{5}{\sqrt{11 - 1}} = \frac{5}{\sqrt{10}} = \frac{5\sqrt{10}}{10} = \frac{\sqrt{10}}{2}$
[2 marks available — 1 mark for substituting 11 into the function, 1 mark for the correct answer]

Answers

4 a) $f(13) = \sqrt{13^2 - 25} = \sqrt{169 - 25} = \sqrt{144} = 12$
[2 marks available — 1 mark for substituting 13 into the function, 1 mark for the correct answer]

b) $f(c) = 2$ so $\sqrt{c^2 - 25} = 2$ *[1 mark]* $\Rightarrow c^2 - 25 = 4$ *[1 mark]*
$\Rightarrow c^2 = 29$ and $c = \pm\sqrt{29}$ *[1 mark]*
[3 marks available in total — as above]

Pages 22-23: Straight Line Graphs

1 a) $4y - 5x = 8$
$4y = 5x + 8$
$y = \frac{5}{4}x + 2$ *[1 mark]* so the gradient is $\frac{5}{4}$ (or 1.25). *[1 mark]*
[2 marks available in total — as above]

b) The y-intercept is c = 2 so the line crosses the y-axis at (0, 2). *[1 mark]*

2 a) Using $y = mx + c$, where m is the gradient, and c is the y-intercept:
$m = \frac{(7 - (-3))}{(5 - 0)} = 2$ *[1 mark]*
When $x = 0$, $y = -3$, so c = –3 *[1 mark]*
So $y = 2x - 3$ *[1 mark]*
[3 marks available in total — as above]

b) Using the gradient from part a), m = 2
When $x = 2$, $y = 10$, so
$10 = (2 \times 2) + c$ *[1 mark]*
i.e. c = 6
So, $y = 2x + 6$ *[1 mark]*
[2 marks available in total — as above]

3 a) Rearrange $3x + 5y = 15$ to give $y = -\frac{3}{5}x + 3$
Find the gradient (m) by comparing to $y = mx + c$:
$m = -\frac{3}{5}$ (or –0.6)
[2 marks available — 1 mark for rearranging the equation, 1 mark for the correct answer]

b) When $y = 0$, $3x = 15$, so $x = 5$. So Q is (5, 0). *[1 mark]*

c) At $x = 0$, $5y = 15$, so $y = 3$. So P is the point (0, 3) *[1 mark]* which means the y-intercept of Line B is 3.
The gradient of Line B is $\frac{(3 - 0)}{(0 - (-1))} = 3$ *[1 mark]*
So the equation of line B is $y = 3x + 3$ *[1 mark]*
[3 marks available in total — as above]

4 $m = \frac{-7 - 17}{5 - (-1)} = -4$
Equation of line is given by $y - a = m(x - b)$, so:
$y - 17 = -4(x - (-1))$
So $y = -4x + 13$
[3 marks available — 1 mark for the correct gradient, 1 mark for using a correct method to find the equation of a line, 1 mark for the correct equation in the form $y = mx + c$]

Page 24: Factorising Quadratics

1 $(y - 4)(y + 6)$ *[1 mark]*

2 a) $(3x + 2)(x - 5)$
[2 marks available — 1 mark for the correct numbers in the brackets, 1 mark for the correct signs]

b) $3x + 2 = 0$ or $x - 5 = 0$
$x = -\frac{2}{3}$ or $x = 5$ *[1 mark]*

3 a) The area of the square is $(x + 3)(x + 3) = x^2 + 6x + 9$
The area of the triangle is $\frac{1}{2}(2x + 2)(x + 3)$
$= \frac{1}{2}(2x^2 + 6x + 2x + 6) = \frac{1}{2}(2x^2 + 8x + 6) = x^2 + 4x + 3$
So the area of the whole shape is $x^2 + 6x + 9 + x^2 + 4x + 3$
$= 2x^2 + 10x + 12$
$2x^2 + 10x + 12 = 60$, so $2x^2 + 10x - 48 = 0$
So $x^2 + 5x - 24 = 0$
[3 marks available — 1 mark for the correct expanded expression for the area of the square, 1 mark for the correct expanded expression for the area of the triangle, 1 mark for setting the total area equal to 60 and rearranging to get the given quadratic]

b) $(x - 3)(x + 8) = 0$ *[1 mark]*
$x - 3 = 0$ or $x + 8 = 0$
$x = 3$ or $x = -8$ *[1 mark for both solutions]*
So $x = 3$ *[1 mark]*
[3 marks available in total — as above]
Taking $x = -8$ would give e.g. $-8 + 3 = -5$ for the length of a side of the square — but lengths can't be negative.

Page 25: The Quadratic Formula

1 $a = 1$, $b = 5$ and $c = 3$
$x = \frac{-5 \pm \sqrt{5^2 - (4 \times 1 \times 3)}}{2 \times 1} = \frac{-5 \pm \sqrt{13}}{2}$
$x = -0.69722...$ or $x = -4.30277...$
$x = -0.70$ or $x = -4.30$
[3 marks available — 1 mark for a correct substitution into the quadratic formula, 1 mark for evaluating the discriminant, 1 mark for both correct solutions]
When you're in the exam, you've always got to write down your unrounded answer before your final rounded one.

2 $a = 2$, $b = -7$ and $c = 2$
$x = \frac{-(-7) \pm \sqrt{(-7)^2 - (4 \times 2 \times 2)}}{2 \times 2} = \frac{7 \pm \sqrt{33}}{4}$
$x = 3.18614...$ or $x = 0.31385...$
$x = 3.19$ or $x = 0.31$
[3 marks available — 1 mark for a correct substitution into the quadratic formula, 1 mark for evaluating the discriminant, 1 mark for both correct solutions]

3 $a = 3$, $b = -2$ and $c = -4$
$x = \frac{-(-2) \pm \sqrt{(2)^2 - (4 \times 3 \times -4)}}{2 \times 3} = \frac{2 \pm \sqrt{52}}{6} = \frac{2 \pm 2\sqrt{13}}{6}$
$x = \frac{1 + \sqrt{13}}{3}$ or $x = \frac{1 - \sqrt{13}}{3}$
[3 marks available — 1 mark for correct substitution into quadratic formula, 1 mark for evaluating discriminant, 1 mark for both correct solutions]

4 $(x + 3)(3x + 3) = 30$
$3x^2 + 12x + 9 = 30$
$3x^2 + 12x - 21 = 0$
$x^2 + 4x - 7 = 0$
$a = 1$, $b = 4$ and $c = -7$
$x = \frac{-4 \pm \sqrt{4^2 - (4 \times 1 \times -7)}}{2 \times 1} = \frac{-4 \pm \sqrt{44}}{2}$
$= \frac{-4 \pm 2\sqrt{11}}{2} = -2 \pm \sqrt{11}$
So the longer side is $3(-2 + \sqrt{11}) + 3 = -3 + 3\sqrt{11}$ cm
[5 marks available — 1 mark for setting up the quadratic equation, 1 mark for the correct substitution, 1 mark for evaluating the discriminant, 1 mark for solvingt the equation and choosing the correct value of x, 1 mark for the correct answer]

Page 26: Completing the Square

1 $(x + 2)^2 - 9 = x^2 + 4x + 4 - 9$ *[1 mark]* $= x^2 + 4x - 5$
$a = 4$ and $b = -5$ *[1 mark]*
[2 marks available in total — as above]

2 $-8 \div 2 = -4$, so $a = -4$ and the bit in brackets is $(x - 4)^2$.
Expanding the brackets: $(x - 4)^2 = x^2 - 8x + 16$.
To complete the square: $6 - 16 = -10$, so $b = -10$.
$x^2 - 8x + 6 = (x - 4)^2 - 10$
[2 marks available — 1 mark for the correct bracket with square, 1 mark for a fully correct answer]

3 a) $-10 \div 2 = -5$, so $p = -5$ and the bit in brackets is $(x - 5)^2$.
Expanding the brackets: $(x - 5)^2 = x^2 - 10x + 25$.
To complete the square: $-5 - 25 = -30$, so $q = -30$.
$p = -5$ and $q = -30$
[2 marks available — 1 mark for the correct bracket with square, 1 mark for a fully correct answer]

b) $(x-5)^2 - 30 = 0$, so $(x-5)^2 = 30$ and $x - 5 = \pm\sqrt{30}$
So $x = 5 + \sqrt{30}$ or $x = 5 - \sqrt{30}$ *[1 mark]*

4 $20 \div 2 = 10$, so the bit in brackets is $(x+10)^2$.
Expanding the brackets: $(x+10)^2 = x^2 + 20x + 100$.
To complete the square: $56 - 100 = -44$, so...
$x^2 + 20x + 56 = (x+10)^2 - 44$
So $x^2 + 20x + 56 = 0 \Rightarrow (x+10)^2 - 44 = 0$
and then $(x+10)^2 = 44 \Rightarrow x + 10 = \pm\sqrt{44} \Rightarrow x = -10 \pm \sqrt{44}$
Simplifying: $x = -10 + 2\sqrt{11}$ or $x = -10 - 2\sqrt{11}$
[4 marks available — 1 mark for the correct bracket with square, 1 mark for completing the square correctly, 1 mark for both correct solutions, 1 mark for both fully simplified solutions]

Pages 27-28: Quadratic Graphs

1 Substituting $x = -4$ and $y = -80$ into $y = nx^2$:
$-80 = n \times (-4)^2 \Rightarrow -80 = 16n \Rightarrow n = -\dfrac{80}{16} = -5$
[2 marks available — 1 mark for substituting (–4, –80) into the equation, 1 mark for the correct answer]

2 a) $r = -6$ *[1 mark]*
   b) $s = 10$ *[1 mark]*
   c) $x = 6$ *[1 mark]*
   d) $y = -(x-6)^2 + 10 = -(x^2 - 12x + 36) + 10 = -x^2 + 12x - 26$
       [2 marks available — 1 mark for correctly expanding the brackets, 1 mark for the correct answer]

3 a) $p = -9$ *[1 mark]*
   b) Substituting $x = 15$ and $y = -30$ into $y = (x-9)^2 + q$:
       $-30 = (15-9)^2 + q \Rightarrow -30 = 36 + q \Rightarrow q = -66$
       [2 marks available — 1 mark for substituting (15, –30) into the equation, 1 mark for the correct answer]
   c) $(9, -66)$ *[1 mark]*

4 Complete the square: $(x-2)^2 = x^2 - 4x + 4$ *[1 mark]*
   $(x-2)^2 + 2 = x^2 - 4x + 6$
   So the completed square is $f(x) = (x-2)^2 + 2$ *[1 mark]*
   So the turning point is $(2, 2)$ *[1 mark]*
   [3 marks available in total — as above]

Page 29: Sketching Quadratic Graphs

1 The turning point has coordinates $(-2, 20)$ and
   the y-intercept is $y = (0+2)^2 + 20 = 4 + 20 = 24$.

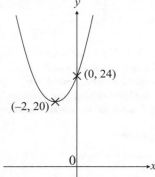

[3 marks available — 1 mark for the correct coordinates of the turning point, 1 mark for sketching a parabola with its turning point consistent with the coordinates calculated, 1 mark for the correct y-intercept]

2 To find intersections with the x-axis, solve $x^2 + 10x - 11 = 0$:
   $(x+11)(x-1) = 0$ so $x = -11, x = 1$
   So the x-intercepts are $(-11, 0)$ and $(1, 0)$.
   To find where the graph crosses the y-axis, substitute $x = 0$
   into the equation: $y = 0 + 0 - 11 = -11$
   So the y-intercept is $(0, -11)$
   Use symmetry and the x-intercepts to find the turning point
   of the curve: $x = \dfrac{1 + (-11)}{2} = -5$
   $y = (-5)^2 + 10(-5) - 11 = -36$
   So the turning point lies at $(-5, -36)$

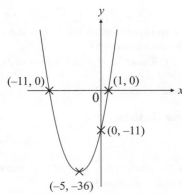

[4 marks available — 1 mark for the correct coordinates of the turning point, 1 mark for sketching a parabola with its turning point consistent with the coordinates calculated, 1 mark for the correct y-intercept, 1 mark for the correct x-intercepts]
You could also find the turning point by completing the square.

Page 30: The Discriminant

1 $a = 10$, $b = -14$, $c = 2$
   Discriminant $= b^2 - 4ac = (-14)^2 - (4 \times 10 \times 2) = 116 > 0$
   Since the discriminant is positive, there are two real, distinct roots.
   [2 marks available — 1 mark for correctly evaluating the discriminant, 1 mark for the correct conclusion]

2 $a = 9$, $b = 6$, $c = 1$
   Discriminant $= 6^2 - (4 \times 9 \times 1) = 0$
   Since the discriminant is zero, the graph of $y = f(x)$ intersects the x-axis exactly once.
   [2 marks available — 1 mark for correctly evaluating the discriminant, 1 mark for the correct conclusion]

3 Discriminant $= k^2 - (4 \times 2 \times k) = k^2 - 8k$
   One real, repeated root $\Rightarrow$ Discriminant $= 0$
   So $k^2 - 8k = 0 \Rightarrow k(k-8) = 0 \Rightarrow k = 0$ or $k = 8$. But $k \neq 0$ so $k = 8$.
   [3 marks available — 1 mark for evaluating the discriminant, 1 mark for setting the discriminant equal to 0, 1 mark for the correct answer]

4 Discriminant $= 4^2 - (4 \times 1 \times p) = 16 - 4p$
   No real solutions means the discriminant is negative.
   So $16 - 4p < 0 \Rightarrow 16 < 4p \Rightarrow p > 4$
   [4 marks available — 1 mark for evaluating the discriminant, 1 mark for setting up the correct inequation, 1 mark for rearranging to 16 < 4p, 1 mark for the correct answer]

Page 31: Algebraic Fractions

1 $\dfrac{x^2 - 4}{x^2 + 8x + 12} = \dfrac{(x+2)(x-2)}{(x+2)(x+6)} = \dfrac{x-2}{x+6}$
   [3 marks available — 1 mark for correctly factorising the denominator, 1 mark for correctly factorising the numerator, 1 mark for the correct answer]

2 $\dfrac{x^2}{3x} \times \dfrac{6}{x+1} = \dfrac{6x^2}{3x(x+1)} = \dfrac{2x}{x+1}$
   [2 marks available — 1 mark for the correct multiplication, 1 mark for the correct answer]

3 $\dfrac{10x}{3+x} \div \dfrac{4}{5(3+x)} = \dfrac{10x}{3+x} \times \dfrac{5(3+x)}{4} = \dfrac{50x(3+x)}{4(3+x)} = \dfrac{50x}{4} = \dfrac{25x}{2}$
   [3 marks available — 1 mark for converting to a multiplication, 1 mark for the correct multiplication, 1 mark for correct answer]

4 $\dfrac{2}{3} + \dfrac{m-2n}{m+3n} = \dfrac{2(m+3n)}{3(m+3n)} + \dfrac{3(m-2n)}{3(m+3n)} = \dfrac{2(m+3n) + 3(m-2n)}{3(m+3n)}$
   $= \dfrac{2m + 6n + 3m - 6n}{3(m+3n)} = \dfrac{5m}{3(m+3n)}$
   [3 marks available — 1 mark for the correct denominator, 1 mark for the correct numerator, 1 mark for the correct simplified final answer]

5 $\dfrac{1}{x-5} + \dfrac{2}{x-2} = \dfrac{x-2}{(x-5)(x-2)} + \dfrac{2(x-5)}{(x-5)(x-2)}$

$= \dfrac{(x-2) + 2(x-5)}{(x-5)(x-2)} = \dfrac{x-2+2x-10}{(x-5)(x-2)} = \dfrac{3x-12}{(x-5)(x-2)}$

[3 marks available — 1 mark for the correct denominator, 1 mark for the correct numerator, 1 mark for the correct simplified final answer]

Pages 32-33: Simultaneous Equations

For all the simultaneous equation questions, you could eliminate the other variable and/or substitute into the other equation — you'll get the marks either way.

1 $x + 3y = 11 \xrightarrow{\times 3} 3x + 9y = 33$

$\begin{array}{ll} 3x + 9y = 33 & x + 3y = 11 \\ \underline{3x + y = 9 -} & x + (3 \times 3) = 11 \\ 8y = 24 & x = 11 - 9 \\ y = 3 & x = 2 \end{array}$

[3 marks available — 1 mark for attempting to scale the equation, 1 mark for a valid strategy to produce a value for x and y, 1 mark for the correct values of x and y]

If you just guess values of x and y and then check to see if they work, you'll get no marks — even if you find the right values. This isn't a valid strategy.

2 $2x + 3y = 12 \xrightarrow{\times 5} 10x + 15y = 60$
$5x + 4y = 9 \xrightarrow{\times 2} 10x + 8y = 18$

$\begin{array}{ll} 10x + 15y = 60 & 2x + 3y = 12 \\ \underline{10x + 8y = 18 -} & 2x = 12 - (3 \times 6) \\ 7y = 42 & 2x = -6 \\ y = 6 & x = -3 \end{array}$

[3 marks available — 1 mark for attempting to scale the equations, 1 mark for a valid strategy to produce a value for x and y, 1 mark for the correct values of x and y]

3 a) Let f be the cost of a chocolate frog and m be the cost of a sugar mouse.
      $4f + 3m = 3.69$ *[1 mark]*

  b) $6f + 2m = 3.96$ *[1 mark]*

  c) $4f + 3m = 3.69 \xrightarrow{\times 2} 8f + 6m = 7.38$
      $6f + 2m = 3.96 \xrightarrow{\times 3} 18f + 6m = 11.88$

$\begin{array}{ll} 18f + 6m = 11.88 & 4f + 3m = 3.69 \\ \underline{8f + 6m = 7.38 -} & 3m = 3.69 - (4 \times 0.45) \\ 10f = 4.5 & 3m = 1.89 \\ f = 0.45 & m = 0.63 \end{array}$

Chocolate frog = 45p (or £0.45)
Sugar mouse = 63p (or £0.63)

[4 marks available — 1 mark for attempting to scale the equations, 1 mark for the correct values of f and m, 1 mark for interpreting the answer as money]

4 a) At P, $y = 0$ so $0 = 18 - 3x$ *[1 mark]* and $3x = 18 \Rightarrow x = 6$.
      The coordinates of point P are $(6, 0)$ *[1 mark]*
      [2 marks available in total — as above]

  b) Point Q is the point where the two lines intersect, so solve the simultaneous equations $y = 18 - 3x$ and $y = 2x - 2$:
      $3x + y = 18$ and $2x - y = 2$
      Adding the equations gives: $5x = 20$, so $x = 4$.
      Substituting this value into $y = 2x - 2$ gives $y = 6$.
      So the coordinates of point Q are $(4, 6)$.
      [2 marks available — 1 mark for a valid strategy to produce a value for x and y, 1 mark for the correct values of x and y]
      You could have done this one by setting the two equations equal to each other and solving for x, then using your x-value to find y.

5 $3x + 5y = 49 \xrightarrow{\times 5} 15x + 25y = 245$
$5x + 2y = 31 \xrightarrow{\times 3} 15x + 6y = 93$

$\begin{array}{ll} 15x + 25y = 245 & 3x + 5y = 49 \\ \underline{15x + 6y = 93 -} & 3x = 49 - (5 \times 8) \\ 19y = 152 & 3x = 9 \\ y = 8 & x = 3 \end{array}$

So R has coordinates $(3, 8)$.

[3 marks available — 1 mark for attempting to scale the equations, 1 mark for a valid strategy to produce a value for x and y, 1 mark for the correct coordinates]

6 Rearrange both equations into the form $ax + by = c$:
  $3y - 4 = 5(x - 2) \Rightarrow 3y - 4 = 5x - 10 \Rightarrow 5x - 3y = 6$
  $3x = 2y + 5 \Rightarrow 3x - 2y = 5$

  $5x - 3y = 6 \xrightarrow{\times 3} 15x - 9y = 18$
  $3x - 2y = 5 \xrightarrow{\times 5} 15x - 10y = 25$

$\begin{array}{ll} 15x - 9y = 18 & 3x = 2y + 5 \\ \underline{15x - 10y = 25 -} & 3x = (2 \times -7) + 5 \\ y = -7 & 3x = -9 \\ & x = -3 \end{array}$

[4 marks available — 1 mark for rearranging the equations, 1 mark for attempting to scale the equations, 1 mark for a valid strategy to produce a value for x and y, 1 mark for the correct values of x and y]

Section Three — Geometric Skills

Page 34: Geometry

1 $5x + (4x - 9°) = 180°$ *[1 mark]*
  Rearranging this: $9x = 189°$
  Therefore $x = 21°$ *[1 mark]*
  $(4y - 12°) + 2y = 180°$ *[1 mark]*
  Rearranging this: $6y = 192°$
  Therefore $y = 32°$ *[1 mark]*
  [4 marks available in total — as above]

2 $OBC = OCB = 27°$
  So $COB = 180° - 27° - 27° = 126°$
  $ADO = 180° - 142° = 38°$
  $OAD = 90°$, so $AOD = 180° - 38° - 90° = 52°$
  Then $AOC = 52° + 126° = 178°$
  [3 marks available — 1 mark for calculating COB, 1 mark for calculating AOD, 1 mark for calculating AOC]
  You should spot that angle OAD is 90° because a radius (OA) is meeting a tangent (EF) at A.

3 $EGA = 180° - 156° = 24°$
  $EAG = BDE = 180° - 119° = 61°$
  $AEG = 180° - 61° - 24° = 95°$
  So $x = 180° - 95° = 85°$
  [3 marks available — 1 mark for calculating EGA, 1 mark for calculating EAG, 1 mark for calculating x]
  There are other ways to do this — as long as you show all your working and give reasons for each step (and get the right answer of course), you'll get full marks.

Pages 35-36: Polygons

1 Triangle ADX is isosceles, so angle DAX = angle $DXA = 41°$ and angle ADC = angle $ADX = 180° - 41° - 41° = 98°$ (angles in a triangle sum to 180°) *[1 mark]*
  Shape $ABCD$ is a kite, so angle ABC = angle $ADC = 98°$ *[1 mark]*
  Sum of angles in a quadrilateral is 360° so
  angle $DAB = 360° - 98° - 53° - 98° = 111°$ *[1 mark]*
  [3 marks available in total — as above]

2 Exterior angle = $180° - 150° = 30°$
  Number of sides = $360° \div 30° = 12$
  [2 marks available — 1 mark for calculating the exterior angle, 1 mark for calculating the number of sides]

3 Exterior angle of a pentagon = 360° ÷ 5 = 72°
Interior angle of a pentagon = 180° − 72° = 108°
Angle in an equilateral triangle = 180° ÷ 3 = 60°
p = 360° − (108° + 60°) *(angles round a point add up to 360°)*
  = 360° − 168° = 192°
[3 marks available — 1 mark for calculating the interior angle of the pentagon, 1 mark for calculating the angle of the triangle, 1 mark for the correct final answer]

4 a) x is the same as an exterior angle, so x = 360° ÷ 8 *[1 mark]*
  x = 45° *[1 mark]*
  [2 marks available in total — as above]

  b) y = (180° − 45°) ÷ 2 *[1 mark]*
  y = 67.5° *[1 mark]*
  [2 marks available in total — as above]

5 a) $DEF + EFG$ = 180° so EFG = 180° − 151° = 29° *[1 mark]*
  AFG = 360° − 224° − 29° = 107° *[1 mark]*
  x = 180° − 107° = 73° *[1 mark]*
  [3 marks available in total — as above]

  b) Sum of interior angles in a hexagon = (6 − 2) × 180°
    = 720° *[1 mark]*
  Sum of the known angles = 117° + 151° + 136° + 73° + 137°
    = 614°
  y = 720° − 614° = 106° *[1 mark]*
  [2 marks available in total — as above]

Pages 37-38: Circle Geometry

There are usually lots of different ways to answer circle geometry questions — you might not have done it the same way we have. Make sure you write down all your working and any angles you find on the way to the final answer.

1 Angle OCA = 90° − 53° = 37°
Angle AOC = 180° − 37° − 37° = 106°
[2 marks available — 1 mark for calculating OCA, 1 mark for the correct final answer]

2 Angle QPR = 90° − 66° = 24°
Angle PQR = 180° − 24° − 90° = 66°
[2 marks available — 1 mark for calculating QPR, 1 mark for the correct final answer]

3 Angle BDF = 180° − 90° − 62° = 28° *[1 mark]*
Angle BDA = angle DBA = 90° − 28° = 62° *[1 mark]*
x = 180° − 2 × 62° = 56° *[1 mark]*
[3 marks available in total — as above]

4 a) Angle ACB = 90° using opposite angles
  Angle BAC = 180° − 90° − 37° = 53°
  [2 marks available — 1 mark for finding ACB, 1 mark for the correct final answer]

  b) Since ACB = 90°, it is the angle in a semi-circle. To be a semi-circle, AB must be the diameter — i.e. it passes through the centre. *[1 mark]*

5 Angle ACO = 24°
Angle BOC = angle AOC = 180° − 90° − 24° = 66°
Reflex angle AOB = 360° − 2 × 66° = 228°
[3 marks available — 1 mark for knowing the triangle AOC contains the same angles as the triangle BOC, 1 mark for calculating the angle BOC or AOC, 1 mark for the correct final answer]

Pages 39-40: Similarity

1 Scale factor = 5 ÷ 2 = 2.5
Enlarged area = 6 × 2.5² = 37.5 cm²
[3 marks available — 1 mark for the correct scale factor, 1 mark for multiplying by the scale factor squared, 1 mark for the correct final answer]
Remember that you have to square the scale factor when you're scaling up areas.

2 a) Scale factor from **A** to **C**:
  n^2 = 108π ÷ 12π = 9
  n = 3 *[1 mark]*
  Volume of **A** = 135π cm³ ÷ 3³ *[1 mark]*
  = 5π cm³ *[1 mark]*
  [3 marks available in total — as above]

  b) Scale factor from **A** to **B**:
  m^2 = 48π ÷ 12π = 4
  m = 2 *[1 mark]*
  Perpendicular height of **B** = 4 cm × 2 *[1 mark]*
  = 8 cm *[1 mark]*
  [3 marks available in total — as above]

3 a) 1.5 m = 150 cm, so the scale factor from the small banner to the large banner = 150 ÷ 30 = 5
  x = 40 ÷ 5 = 8 cm
  [2 marks available — 1 mark for the correct scale factor, 1 mark for the correct answer]

  b) 0.6 ÷ (5)² = 0.024 m²
  [2 marks available — 1 mark for using the correct scale factor (5²), 1 mark for the correct answer]

4 a) The scale factor from ABE to CDE = 18 ÷ 4.5 = 4
  CE = 12 ÷ 4 = 3 cm
  [2 marks available — 1 mark for the correct scale factor, 1 mark for the correct answer]

  b) Let x be the length of ED.
  So EB = 4x = x + 10
  So 3x = 10 $\Rightarrow$ x = $\frac{10}{3}$ cm
  [2 marks available — 1 mark for forming an equation using the scale factor from a), 1 mark for the correct answer]

5 a) The scale factor from ABC to ACD = 8 ÷ 6 = $\frac{4}{3}$
  x = 6 ÷ $\frac{4}{3}$ = 4.5 cm
  y = 3 × $\frac{4}{3}$ = 4 cm
  [3 marks available — 1 mark for the correct scale factor, 1 mark for the correct value of x, 1 mark for the correct value of y]

  b) Area of ACD = 9 × $\left(\frac{4}{3}\right)^2$ = 16 cm²
  So area of $ABCD$ = 9 + 16 = 25 cm²
  [2 marks available — 1 mark for using the correct scale factor $\left(\frac{4}{3}\right)^2$, 1 mark for the correct final answer]

6 Scale factor = 50 ÷ 40 = 1.25
Price of smaller bag = 10 ÷ 1.25³ = £5.12
[3 marks available — 1 mark for the correct scale factor, 1 mark for dividing by the scale factor cubed, 1 mark for the correct answer]

Pages 41-42: Arcs and Sectors

1 a) Area of sector = $\frac{30°}{360°}$ × π × 6² = 3π = 9.4247...
    = 9.42 cm² (3 s.f.)
  [3 marks available — 1 mark for the correct fraction, 1 mark for the correct substitution into the formula, 1 mark for the correct answer]

  b) Arc length = $\frac{30°}{360°}$ × 2 × π × 6 = π
  Perimeter (2 × 6) + π = 12 + π = 15.1415... = 15.1 cm (3 s.f.)
  [3 marks available — 1 mark for the correct substitution into the formula, 1 mark for the correct arc length, 1 mark for the correct answer]

2 Reflex angle = 360° − 143° = 217°
Area of major sector = $\frac{217°}{360°}$ × π × 11.2² = 237.543...
    = 237.5 cm² (1 d.p.)

[3 marks available — 1 mark for the correct fraction, 1 mark for correct substitution into formula, 1 mark for the correct answer]

3 Arc length $= 10.3 = \frac{49.1°}{360°} \times \pi \times d$ so $d = \frac{10.3 \times 360}{49.1 \times \pi}$
$$= 24.0385... = 24 \text{ cm (3 s.f)}$$

[3 marks available — 1 mark for the correct expression for the arc length, 1 mark for rearranging for the diameter, 1 mark for the correct answer]

4 Call the angle in the sector x.
Arc length $= 3 = \frac{x}{360°} \times 2 \times \pi \times 6.8$

So $x = \frac{3 \times 360}{2 \times 6.8 \times \pi} = 25.277...°$

Area of smaller sector $= \frac{25.277...°}{360°} \times \pi \times 6.8^2 = 10.2 \text{ cm}^2$

Area of larger sector $= \frac{25.277...°}{360°} \times \pi \times 14.4^2 = 45.741... \text{ cm}^2$

Total area $= 10.2 + 45.741... = 55.9 \text{ cm}^2$ (3 s.f.)

[5 marks available — 1 mark for the correct expression for the arc length, 1 mark for the correct angle of the sectors, 1 mark for the correct area of the small sector, 1 mark for the correct area of the large sector, 1 mark for the correct final answer]

5 Each straight section $= 2 \times$ radius $= 2 \times 9 = 18$ cm *[1 mark]*
Each curved section $= \frac{1}{3} \times$ circumference of circle
$$= \frac{1}{3} \times 2 \times \pi \times 9 \text{ [1 mark]}$$
$$= 6\pi \text{ cm [1 mark]}$$
Total length $= 3 \times 18 + 3 \times 6\pi = 110.548...$
$$= 110.5 \text{ cm (1 d.p.) [1 mark]}$$

[4 marks available in total — as above]

Pages 43-44: Volume

1 Volume of pool $= \pi \times (2 \div 2)^2 \times 0.4 = 0.4\pi \text{ m}^3$ *[1 mark]*
Volume of water Amy should use $= 0.4\pi \times \frac{3}{4}$ *[1 mark]*
$= 0.94 \text{ m}^3$ (2 d.p.) *[1 mark]*
[3 marks available in total — as above]

2 A regular hexagon is made up of 6 identical triangles.
Area of triangle $= \frac{1}{2} \times 8 \times 7 = 28 \text{ cm}^2$ *[1 mark]*
Area of whole hexagon cross-section $= 28 \times 6 = 168 \text{ cm}^2$ *[1 mark]*
Volume of prism = cross-sectional area $\times$ length
$$= 168 \times 6 = 1008 \text{ cm}^3 \text{ [1 mark]}$$
[3 marks available in total — as above]

3 Volume of cone $= \frac{1}{3}(\pi \times 6^2 \times 18) = 216\pi \text{ cm}^3$ *[1 mark]*

So $\frac{4}{3}\pi r^3 = 216\pi \text{ cm}^3$ *[1 mark]*
$r^3 = 162$ *[1 mark]*
$r = 5.4513... \text{ cm} = 5.45 \text{ cm}$ (3 s.f.) *[1 mark]*
[4 marks available in total — as above]

4 Volume of hemisphere $= \frac{2}{3} \times \pi \times 7^3 = \frac{686}{3}\pi \text{ cm}^3$
Volume of cone $= \frac{1}{3} \times \pi \times 2^2 \times 2\sqrt{35} = 49.562... \text{ cm}^3$

Total volume $= \frac{686}{3}\pi + 49.562... = 767.9399... = 768 \text{ cm}^3$ (3 s.f.)

[5 marks available — 1 mark for correctly substituting into the formula for the volume of a hemisphere, 1 mark for correctly substituting into the formula for the volume of a cone, 1 mark for adding volumes, 1 mark for all calculations carried out correctly, 1 mark for the correct answer rounded to 3 s.f.]

5 Volume $= \frac{1}{2} \times (\frac{4}{3} \times \pi \times 9^3) - \frac{1}{2} \times (\frac{4}{3} \times \pi \times 8^3)$
$$= 1526.814... - 1072.330... = 454 \text{ cm}^3 \text{ (3 s.f.)}$$

[4 marks available — 1 mark for correctly substituting into the formula for the volume of both hemispheres, 1 mark for subtracting volumes, 1 mark for all calculations carried out correctly, 1 mark for the correct final answer rounded to 3 s.f.]
You still get full marks if you simplified the volume before multiplying everything through — e.g. you got $\frac{2}{3}\pi(729 - 512)$.

6 Volume of removed cone $= \frac{1}{3} \times \pi \times 12.5^2 \times 250 = 40906.154...$
Volume of full cone $= \frac{1}{3} \times \pi \times 15^2 \times (250 + 50) = 70685.834...$
Volume of silo $= 70685.834... - 40906.154... = 29779.68...$
$$= 29\,800 \text{ m}^3 \text{ (3 s.f.)}$$

[5 marks available — 1 mark for correctly substituting into the formula for the volume of the removed cone, 1 mark for correctly substituting into the formula for the volume of the full cone, 1 mark for attempting to find the difference in the volumes, 1 mark for all calculations carried out correctly, 1 mark for the correct answer rounded to 3 s.f.]

Pages 45-47: Pythagoras' Theorem

1 $3.5^2 = x^2 + 2.1^2$
$x = \sqrt{12.25 - 4.41} = \sqrt{7.84}$
$x = 2.8$ m
[2 marks available — 1 mark for correct substitution into Pythagoras' theorem, 1 mark for the correct answer]

2 Let x be the height of the triangle:
$13^2 = 5^2 + x^2$
$x = \sqrt{169 - 25} = \sqrt{144}$
$x = 12$
Area $= \frac{1}{2} \times 10 \times 12 = 60 \text{ cm}^2$
[3 marks available — 1 mark for correct substitution into Pythagoras' theorem, 1 mark for the correct value of x, 1 mark for the correct area]

3 Length of EA:
$28.3^2 = 20^2 + EA^2$
$EA = \sqrt{800.89 - 400} = 20.02...$
Length of CE:
$54.3^2 = 20^2 + CE^2$
$CE = \sqrt{2948.49 - 400} = 50.48...$
Perimeter $= 28.3 + 54.3 + EA + CE = 153.1$ cm (1 d.p)
[4 marks available — 1 mark for correct substitution into Pythagoras' theorem to find EA or CE, 1 mark for the correct value of EA, 1 mark for the correct value of CE, 1 mark for correct perimeter to the specified degree of accuracy]

4 Difference in x-coordinates $= 8 - 2 = 6$
Difference in y-coordinates $= 8 - -1 = 9$
So length of line segment $= \sqrt{6^2 + 9^2} = \sqrt{36 + 81}$
$= \sqrt{117} = \sqrt{9 \times 13} = 3\sqrt{13}$
[3 marks available — 1 mark for both correct differences in coordinates, 1 mark for correct substitution into Pythagoras' theorem, 1 mark for correct answer]

5 If the sections meet at a right-angle, Pythagoras' theorem means that $30^2 + 75^2 = h^2$.
$30^2 + 75^2 = 6525, \ h^2 = 85^2 = 7225$
$6525 \neq 7225$ so the sections do not meet at a right-angle.
[3 marks available — 1 mark for using the converse of Pythagoras' theorem, 1 mark for correctly evaluating $30^2 + 75^2$ and h^2, 1 mark for comparison and correct conclusion]

6 To find the height of the badge, you first need to find the height, a, of the isosceles triangle formed by two radii and a chord:

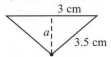

So $a^2 + 3^2 = 3.5^2$
$a^2 = 3.5^2 - 3^2 = 3.25$
$a = \sqrt{3.25}$ cm
As the chords are the same length, the other isosceles triangle formed will have the same height. So the total height of the shape, $h = 2 \times \sqrt{3.25} = 3.60555.. = 3.61$ cm (3 s.f.)
[4 marks available — 1 mark for identifying the right-angled triangle, 1 mark for a correct equation involving Pythagoras, 1 mark for the correct value of a, 1 mark for the correct final answer to the specified degree of accuracy]

7 $OH^2 = 6^2 + 3^2 + 4^2 = 61$
$OH = \sqrt{61} = 7.81024... = 7.81$ (3 s.f.)
[3 marks available — 1 mark for correct substitution into Pythagoras' theorem in 3D, 1 mark for the correct value of OH^2, 1 mark for the correct final answer to to 3 s.f.]

8 Consider the circular cross-section at the centre of the snow globe:

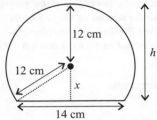

To find h, you need to find the vertical height x in the triangle shown using Pythagoras' theorem.
$(14 \div 2)^2 + x^2 = 12^2$ so $x^2 = 12^2 - 7^2 = 95$
$x = \sqrt{95} = 9.746...$
The height of the snow globe is $h = 12 + 9.746... = 21.746...$
$= 21.7$ cm (3 s.f.)

[4 marks available — 1 mark for identifying the right-angled triangle, 1 mark for a correct equation involving Pythagoras, 1 mark for the correct value of x, 1 mark for the correct height to the specified degree of accuracy]

Page 48: 3D Coordinates

1 The radius of the globe is 1 so $N(0, 0, 1)$ and $W(0, -1, 0)$.
[2 marks available — 1 mark for the correct coordinates of N, 1 mark for the correct coordinates of W]

2 The cube has sides of length 4 so $B(4, 0, 3)$ and $C(0, 4, 7)$.
[2 marks available — 1 mark for the correct coordinates of B, 1 mark for the correct coordinates of C]

3 The y-coordinate of the midpoint of the base is $8 \div 2 = 4$ so $M(3, 4, 0)$.
The x-coordinate of B is $2 \times 3 = 6$ so $B(6, 0, 0)$.
[2 marks available — 1 mark for the correct coordinates of M, 1 mark for the correct coordinates of B]

Pages 49-50: Vectors

1 a) $\begin{pmatrix} -3 \\ 5 \end{pmatrix} - \begin{pmatrix} 5 \\ 4 \end{pmatrix} = \begin{pmatrix} -8 \\ 1 \end{pmatrix}$ *[1 mark]*

b) $4 \times \begin{pmatrix} 5 \\ 4 \end{pmatrix} - \begin{pmatrix} -4 \\ -6 \end{pmatrix} = \begin{pmatrix} 20 \\ 16 \end{pmatrix} - \begin{pmatrix} -4 \\ -6 \end{pmatrix} = \begin{pmatrix} 24 \\ 22 \end{pmatrix}$
[2 marks available — 1 mark for multiplying correctly by a scalar, 1 mark for the correct answer]

c) $2 \times \begin{pmatrix} -3 \\ 5 \end{pmatrix} + \begin{pmatrix} 5 \\ 4 \end{pmatrix} + 3 \times \begin{pmatrix} -4 \\ -6 \end{pmatrix} = \begin{pmatrix} -6 \\ 10 \end{pmatrix} + \begin{pmatrix} 5 \\ 4 \end{pmatrix} + \begin{pmatrix} -12 \\ -18 \end{pmatrix}$
$= \begin{pmatrix} -13 \\ -4 \end{pmatrix}$
$\left| \begin{pmatrix} -13 \\ -4 \end{pmatrix} \right| = \sqrt{(-13)^2 + (-4)^2} = \sqrt{185} = 13.6...$
[4 marks available — 1 mark for all scalar multiplications correct, 1 mark for correct evaluation of the resultant vector, 1 mark for knowing how to find the magnitude, 1 mark for the correct answer]

2 $4\mathbf{a} + 3\mathbf{b}$ *[1 mark]*

3 $\overrightarrow{OM} = \overrightarrow{OA} + \overrightarrow{AM} = \overrightarrow{OA} + \frac{1}{2}\overrightarrow{AB}$ *[1 mark]*
$\overrightarrow{AB} = \mathbf{b} - 2\mathbf{a}$ or $-2\mathbf{a} + \mathbf{b}$
$\overrightarrow{OM} = 2\mathbf{a} + \frac{1}{2}(-2\mathbf{a} + \mathbf{b})$ or $\overrightarrow{OM} = 2\mathbf{a} + \frac{1}{2}(\mathbf{b} - 2\mathbf{a})$
$= \mathbf{a} + \frac{1}{2}\mathbf{b}$ *[1 mark]*
[2 marks available in total — as above]

4

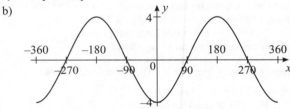

$\overrightarrow{BD} = \overrightarrow{BA} + \overrightarrow{AD} = \begin{pmatrix} -4 \\ 1 \end{pmatrix} + \begin{pmatrix} 7 \\ 2 \end{pmatrix} = \begin{pmatrix} 3 \\ 3 \end{pmatrix}$
So the magnitude of $\overrightarrow{BD}$ is $\sqrt{3^2 + 3^2} = 4.24264... = 4.24$ (2 d.p.)
[3 marks available — 1 mark for adding vectors together correctly, 1 mark for knowing how to find the magnitude, 1 mark for the correct answer]

5 a) $\overrightarrow{CD} = -2\mathbf{a}$ *[1 mark]*
b) $\overrightarrow{AC} = 2\mathbf{d} + 2\mathbf{a}$ *[1 mark]*
c) $\overrightarrow{BL} = \overrightarrow{BA} + \frac{1}{2}\overrightarrow{AC} = -2\mathbf{a} + (\mathbf{d} + \mathbf{a}) = \mathbf{d} - \mathbf{a}$ *[1 mark]*

6 $|\mathbf{u}| = \sqrt{5^2 + (-2)^2 + (-4)^2} = \sqrt{45} = \sqrt{9 \times 5} = 3\sqrt{5}$
[2 marks available — 1 mark for knowing how to find the magnitude, 1 mark for the correct simplified answer]

7 $\mathbf{r} = \begin{pmatrix} 3 \\ 4 \end{pmatrix}$, $\mathbf{s} = \begin{pmatrix} 0 \\ 3 \end{pmatrix}$ and so $\mathbf{r} + \mathbf{s} = \begin{pmatrix} 3 \\ 7 \end{pmatrix}$
Then $|\mathbf{r} + \mathbf{s}| = \sqrt{3^2 + 7^2} = \sqrt{58} = 7.6157...$
*[4 marks available — 1 mark for stating the component form of **r** or **s**, 1 mark for stating the other vector and correct **r** + **s**, 1 mark for knowing how to find the magnitude, 1 mark for the correct answer]*

Section Four — Trigonometric Skills

Page 51: Trigonometric Graphs

1 $p = -1$, $q = 3$
[2 marks available — 1 mark for the correct value of p, 1 mark for the correct value of q]

2 a) $90°$ *[1 mark]*
b)

[3 marks available — 1 mark for the correct sin shape in the range required, 1 mark for the correct amplitude, 1 mark for the correct translation]

c) $f(x) = -4 \cos x$ *[1 mark]*
You can see from the graph that $f(x)$ is $y = \cos x$ reflected in the x-axis and stretched by a scale factor of 4.

3 a) $g(x) = \tan 5x$ *[1 mark]*
b) $f(x)$ is undefined at $x = 90, 270, 450, ...$
So $g(x)$ is undefined at $x = 90 \div 5 = 18$,
$x = 270 \div 5 = 54$,
$x = 450 \div 5 = 90$.
[3 marks available — 1 mark for using the correct undefined points of f(x), 1 mark for dividing by 5, 1 mark for all 3 correct values of x]

Page 52: Trigonometry — Sin, Cos, Tan

1 $\tan 58° = \dfrac{XY}{4}$ *[1 mark]* $\Rightarrow XY = 4 \tan 58° = 6.40133...$ *[1 mark]*
$\cos 55° = \dfrac{YZ}{6.40133...}$ *[1 mark]* $\Rightarrow YZ = 6.40133... \times \cos 55°$
$= 3.6716...$
$= 3.67$ (2 d.p.) *[1 mark]*

[4 marks available in total — as above]

2 a) $\tan x = \frac{6}{9}$ *[1 mark]*

$x = \tan^{-1}\left(\frac{6}{9}\right) = 33.7°$ (1 d.p) *[1 mark]*

[2 marks available in total — as above]

b) *EG bisects the angle FEH, so find angle FEM:*

$\tan x = \frac{6}{5}$ *[1 mark]*

$x = \tan^{-1}\left(\frac{6}{5}\right) = 50.19...°$ *[1 mark]*

$FEH = 50.19...° \times 2 = 100.388... = 100.4°$ (1 d.p) *[1 mark]*

[3 marks available in total — as above]

3 Call the distance from the centre of the circle to the centre of an edge, x. The radius bisects the internal angle forming angle a.

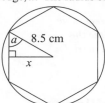

Sum of the internal angles of a hexagon = $(6-2) \times 180° = 720°$
Each internal angle of a hexagon = $720° \div 6 = 120°$ *[1 mark]*
$a = 120° \div 2 = 60°$ *[1 mark]*
$\sin 60° = \frac{x}{8.5}$ *[1 mark]*
$x = 8.5 \times \sin 60° = 7.3612... = 7.36$ cm (2 d.p) *[1 mark]*
[4 marks available in total — as above]
You could also use the calculation cos 30° × 8.5 to find the value of x. As long as you make sure you show your working, you'll get full marks if your answer is correct.

Page 53: Related Angles

1 Use the graph of $y = \cos x$:

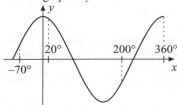

cos 200°, cos (−70)°, cos 20°, cos 360° *[1 mark]*

2 $x = 360 - 130 = 230$ *[1 mark]*

3 The other value of x is $180° - 60° = 120°$ *[1 mark]*

4 Using the symmetry of the graph, $x = 180 - 18 = 162$ *[1 mark]*
and $x = 360 - 18 = 342$ *[1 mark]*
[2 marks available in total — as above]

Pages 54-55: Solving Trig Equations

1 $x = \cos^{-1}(0.65) = 49.458...° = 49.5°$ (1 d.p.) *[1 mark]*
Using the C quadrant in the CAST diagram, the other value of x is
$x = 360° - 49.458...° = 310.541...° = 310.5°$ (1 d.p.) *[1 mark]*
[2 marks available in total — as above]
If you're not comfortable with the CAST diagram, don't forget you can sketch the relevant trig graph to make sure you include all the solutions in the given interval.

2 Rearrange the equation to get sin x on its own:
$5 \sin x = -2 \Rightarrow \sin x = -\frac{2}{5} = -0.4$ *[1 mark]*
$x = \sin^{-1}(-0.4) = -23.5781...°$
Since x is negative, use the T and C quadrants
in the CAST diagram:
$x = 180° + 23.5781...° = 203.6°$ (1 d.p.) *[1 mark]*
$x = 360° - 23.5781...° = 336.4°$ (1 d.p.) *[1 mark]*
[3 marks available in total — as above]

3 $-\sin x + 2 = \frac{3}{2} \Rightarrow \sin x = \frac{1}{2}$

$x = \sin^{-1}\left(\frac{1}{2}\right) = 30$

$x = 180 - 30 = 150$
[4 marks available — 1 mark for setting up an equation, 1 mark for rearranging to make sin x the subject, 1 mark for the first correct solution, 1 mark for the second correct solution]

4 a) $d = 24 + 21 \sin 70° = 43.7335... = 43.7$ m (1 d.p.) *[1 mark]*

b) The maximum value of sin x is 1 so the
maximum value of d is $24 + 21 = 45$ m *[1 mark]*

c) From b), $d = 45$ at the top of the circle.
When $x = 0°$, $\sin x = 0$, so $d = 24$.
Therefore, the radius of the circular lap is $45 - 24 = 21$ m.
The circumference of the lap is $2 \times \pi \times 21 = 131.9468...$
$= 131.9$ m (1 d.p).
[2 marks available — 1 mark for the correct radius, 1 mark for the correct answer]

d) $12 = 24 + 21 \sin x \Rightarrow -12 = 21 \sin x \Rightarrow \sin x = -\frac{4}{7}$
$x = \sin^{-1}\left(-\frac{4}{7}\right) = -34.8499...°$
Since x is negative, use the T and C quadrants
in the CAST diagram:
$x = 180° + 34.8499...° = 215°$ (to the nearest degree)
$x = 360° - 34.8499...° = 325°$ (to the nearest degree)
[4 marks available — 1 mark for correctly substituting 12 into the equation, 1 mark for rearranging to make sin x the subject, 1 mark for the first correct solution, 1 mark for the second correct solution]

Page 56: Trig Identities

1 $\sin^2 x + \cos^2 x \equiv 1$, so
$2(1 - \cos x) = 3 \sin^2 x \Rightarrow 2(1 - \cos x) = 3(1 - \cos^2 x)$
$\Rightarrow 2 - 2 \cos x = 3 - 3\cos^2 x$
$\Rightarrow 3\cos^2 x - 2 \cos x - 1 = 0$
[2 marks available — 1 mark for writing sin² x in terms of cos² x, 1 mark for a fully correct argument with no errors]

2 $\sin^2 x + \cos^2 x \equiv 1$, so
$\sin^2 x \tan x \equiv (1 - \cos^2 x)\tan x$
$\equiv \tan x - \cos^2 x \tan x$
$\equiv \tan x - \cos^2 x \, \frac{\sin x}{\cos x}$
$\equiv \tan x - \sin x \cos x$ as required
[3 marks available — 1 mark for writing sin² x in terms of cos² x, 1 mark for writing tan x in terms of sin x and cos x, 1 mark for a fully correct argument with no errors]

3 a) $f(x) = \frac{\sin^3 x}{\cos x} + \sin x \cos x \equiv \frac{\sin^3 x + \sin x \cos^2 x}{\cos x}$ *[1 mark]*

$\equiv \frac{\sin x(\sin^2 x + \cos^2 x)}{\cos x}$ *[1 mark]*

$\equiv \frac{\sin x}{\cos x}$ *[1 mark]*

$\equiv \tan x$ *[1 mark]*

[4 marks available in total — as above]

b) $5f(x) = 10$ is equivalent to $5 \tan x = 10 \Rightarrow \tan x = 2$
$x = \tan^{-1}(2) = 63.4349...° = 63.4°$ (1 d.p.)
Using the T quadrant in the CAST diagram:
$x = 180° + 63.4349...° = 243.4°$ (1 d.p.)
[3 marks available — 1 mark for making tan x the subject, 1 mark for the first correct solution, 1 mark for the second correct solution]

Pages 57-58: The Sine and Cosine Rules

1 Area $= \frac{1}{2} \times 14 \times 12 \times 0.9$ *[1 mark]* $= 75.6$ cm² *[1 mark]*
[2 marks available in total — as above]

2 a) $AC^2 = 10^2 + 7^2 - (2 \times 10 \times 7 \times \cos 85°) = 136.7981...$
$AC = 11.6960... = 11.7$ cm (3 s.f)
[3 marks available — 1 mark for correct substitution into the cosine rule, 1 mark for evaluating AC², 1 mark for the correct value of AC]

b) Area $= \frac{1}{2} \times 10 \times 7 \times \sin 85°$ *[1 mark]*

$= 34.8668... = 34.9$ cm^2 (3 s.f) *[1 mark]*

[2 marks available in total — as above]

3 $\dfrac{36}{\sin 112°} = \dfrac{17}{\sin ACB}$ *[1 mark]*

$\sin ACB = \dfrac{17 \times \sin 112°}{36}$ *[1 mark]*

$ACB = \sin^{-1}\left(\dfrac{17 \times \sin 112°}{36}\right) = 25.9659... = 26.0°$ *[1 mark]*

[3 marks available in total — as above]

4 $BC^2 = (2x)^2 + (3x)^2 - (2 \times 2x \times 3x \times \cos 60°)$

$= 4x^2 + 9x^2 - 6x^2 = 7x^2$

$BC = \sqrt{7x^2} = x\sqrt{7}$ cm

Perimeter of $ABC = 2x + 3x + x\sqrt{7} = (5 + \sqrt{7})x$ cm so $a = 5$, $b = 7$

[4 marks available — 1 mark for correct substitution into the cosine rule, 1 mark for evaluating BC^2, 1 mark for the correct value of BC, 1 mark for the correct values of a and b]

5 Angle $ABD = 180° - 90° - 31° - 12° = 47°$

Angle $ACB = 180° - 12° - 47° = 121°$ *[1 mark for both]*

Use the sine rule: $\dfrac{3.3}{\sin 12°} = \dfrac{AB}{\sin 121°}$

$AB = \dfrac{3.3}{\sin 12°} \times \sin 121°$ *[1 mark]* $= 13.6050...$ m *[1 mark]*

Find length BD: $\cos 47° = \dfrac{BD}{13.6050...}$

$BD = \cos 47° \times 13.6050...$ *[1 mark]*

$BD = 9.2786... = 9.28$ m (3 s.f.) *[1 mark]*

[5 marks available in total — as above]

There's more than one way of doing this question. As long as you've used a correct method to get the right answer you'll still get the marks.

6 Area of triangle $ACD = \frac{1}{2} \times 60 \times 80 = 2400$ cm^2

Using Pythagoras' theorem:

$AC^2 = 60^2 + 80^2 = 10\,000$ so $AC = 100$

Area of triangle $ABC = \frac{1}{2} \times 70 \times 100 \times \sin 61° = 3061.16...$ cm^2

Area of $ABCD = 2400 + 3061.16... = 5461.16... = 5461$ cm^2 (4 s.f.)

[5 marks available — 1 mark for substituting correctly into the formula for the area of ACD, 1 mark for substituting correctly into Pythagoras' theorem, 1 mark for the correct length of AC, 1 mark for substituting correctly into the formula for the area of ABC, 1 mark for the correct final answer]

Page 59: Trigonometry with Bearings

1 a)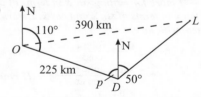

Using allied angles, angle $p = 180° - 110° = 70°$.

So $ODL = 70° + 50° = 120°$ *[1 mark]*

Using the sine rule: $\dfrac{390}{\sin 120°} = \dfrac{225}{\sin OLD}$ *[1 mark]*

$\sin OLD = \dfrac{225 \times \sin 120°}{390}$

$OLD = \sin^{-1}\left(\dfrac{225 \times \sin 120°}{390}\right) = 29.9755...°$ *[1 mark]*

So $DOL = 180° - 120° - 29.9755...° = 30.0244...°$

The bearing from O to L is $110° - 30.0244...° = 79.97...°$

$= 080°$ *[1 mark]*

[4 marks available in total — as above]

b) Using the cosine rule:

$DL^2 = 225^2 + 390^2 - 2 \times 225 \times 390 \times \cos 30.0244...°$

$= 50\,775.07...$

$DL = 225.33... = 225$ km (3 s.f.)

[3 marks available — 1 mark for correct substitution into the cosine rule, 1 mark for evaluating DL^2, 1 mark for the correct value of DL]

You could also use the sine rule to find the length of DL.

2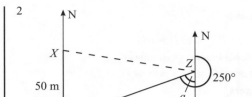

Angle $q = 250° - 180° = 70°$

Using alternate angles, $XYZ = 70°$

Using the cosine rule:

$XZ^2 = 50^2 + 100^2 - 2 \times 50 \times 100 \times \cos 70° = 9079.798...$

$XZ = 95.287... = 95.3$ m (3 s.f.)

[4 marks available — 1 mark for the correct value of XYZ, 1 mark for correct substitution into the cosine rule, 1 mark for evaluating XZ^2, 1 mark for the correct value of XZ]

Section Five — Statistical Skills

Pages 60-61: Comparing Data Sets

1 In ascending order: 1, 2, 2, 4, 5, 6, 7

Median = 4

Lower quartile = 2, upper quartile = 6

Semi-interquartile range $= (6 - 2) \div 2 = 2$

[3 marks available — 1 mark for the correct median, 1 mark for both correct quartiles, 1 mark for the correct semi-interquartile range]

2 Mean $= \overline{x} = (6 + 12 + 10 + 1 + 0 + 9 + 4) \div 7 = 42 \div 7 = 6$

$(x - \overline{x})^2 = 0,\ 36,\ 16,\ 25,\ 36,\ 9,\ 4$

$\Sigma (x - \overline{x})^2 = 126$

Standard deviation $= \sqrt{\dfrac{126}{6}} = \sqrt{21}$

So $c = 21$

[4 marks available — 1 mark for the correct mean and all values of $(x - \overline{x})^2$, 1 mark for substituting correctly into the formula, 1 mark for the correct final answer]

You might have used the other formula for the standard deviation — it gives the same answer.

3 a) In ascending order: 3, 4, 4, 5, 7, 7

Lower quartile = 4, upper quartile = 7

Semi-interquartile range $= (7 - 4) \div 2 = 1.5$

[2 marks available — 1 mark for both correct quartiles, 1 mark for the correct semi-interquartile range]

b) $\overline{x} = (7 + 3 + 5 + 4 + 7 + 4) \div 6 = 30 \div 6 = 5$

$(x - \overline{x})^2 = 4,\ 4,\ 0,\ 1,\ 4,\ 1$

$\Sigma (x - \overline{x})^2 = 14$

Standard deviation $= \sqrt{\dfrac{14}{5}} = 1.6733... = 1.67$ (2 d.p.)

[3 marks available — 1 mark for the correct mean and all values of $(x - \overline{x})^2$ correct, 1 mark for substituting correctly into the formula, 1 mark for the correct final answer]

c) The semi-interquartile range will be less affected since 80 is an extreme value and the standard deviation is affected more by extreme values. *[1 mark]*

4 a) In ascending order: 8, 8, 9, 12, 13, 14, 14, 16, 18, 19, 22

Median = 14

Lower quartile = 9, upper quartile = 18

Semi-interquartile range $= (18 - 9) \div 2 = 4.5$

[3 marks available — 1 mark for the correct median, 1 mark for both correct quartiles, 1 mark for the correct semi-interquartile range]

b) On average, more strawberries were collected from patch A. The number of strawberries collected from patch B was more consistent.
[2 marks available — 1 mark for correct comparison of medians, 1 mark for correct comparison of semi-interquartile ranges]
When comparing data, remember a greater median or mean means the data was larger on average/overall. A greater semi-interquartile range or standard deviation means a larger spread, so the data is more varied/less consistent

5 a) Mean = $\overline{x} = (22 + 20 + 16 + 3 + 15 + 31 + 22 + 15) \div 8 = 18$
$(x - \overline{x})^2 = 16, 4, 4, 225, 9, 169, 16, 9$
$\sum(x - \overline{x})^2 = 452$
Standard deviation = $\sqrt{\dfrac{452}{7}} = 8.0356... = 8.04$ (3 s.f.)
[4 marks available — 1 mark for the correct mean, 1 mark for all values of (x − $\overline{x}$)² correct, 1 mark for substituting correctly into the formula, 1 mark for the correct final answer]

b) On average, there were fewer children at the parties in the first month. The number of children at the parties was less consistent in the first month.
[2 marks available — 1 mark for correct comparison of means, 1 mark for correct comparison of standard deviations]

Pages 62-63: Scattergraphs

1 a)
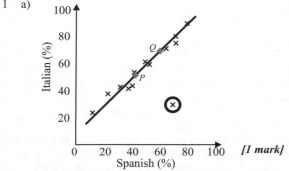
[1 mark]

b) Strong positive correlation *[1 mark]*

c) Gradient = m = $\dfrac{70 - 52}{61 - 43} = 1$
$I - 70 = 1(S - 61) \Rightarrow I = S + 9$
[3 marks available — 1 mark for the correct gradient, 1 mark for substituting the gradient and a point into a correct formula, 1 mark for the correct equation in the form I = mS + c]

d) Italian result = $y = 37 + 9 = 46\%$ *[1 mark]*

2 Gradient = $\dfrac{44 - 19}{5 - 10} = -5$
$y - 44 = -5(x - 5) \Rightarrow y - 44 = -5x + 25 \Rightarrow y = -5x + 69$
Customers on Day 3 = $-5 \times 3 + 69 = 54$
[4 marks available — 1 mark for the correct gradient, 1 mark for substituting the gradient and a point into a correct formula, 1 mark for the correct equation, 1 mark for the correct estimate]

3 a) As the amount spent on advertising increases, so does the value of sales. *[1 mark]*
Or you could say there's a positive correlation between the amount spent and the value of sales.

b) Gradient = $\dfrac{170 - 60}{1.85 - 0.15} = \dfrac{110}{1.7}$
$S - 60 = \dfrac{110}{1.7}(A - 0.15) \Rightarrow 1.7S - 102 = 110A - 16.5$
$\Rightarrow 17S - 1100A - 855 = 0$
[3 marks available — 1 mark for the correct gradient, 1 mark for substituting the gradient and a point into a correct formula, 1 mark for a correct equation in the required form]

c) $17S - 1100 \times 0.6 - 855 = 0 \Rightarrow S = 89.117...$
So £89 100 (3 s.f.)
[2 marks available — 1 mark for correctly substituting 0.6 into the equation, 1 mark for the correct answer]

d) The predication may not be reliable *[1 mark]* as the spend on advertising is beyond the range of the data (i.e. $A = 3 > 1.85$, the largest value of A in the data set) *[1 mark]*.
[2 marks available in total — as above]

Practice Paper 1

1 $4 = \dfrac{1}{2}y + 2x \Rightarrow 8 = y + 4x \Rightarrow y = -4x + 8$
So the gradient is –4.
[2 marks available — 1 mark for rewriting as y = mx + c, 1 mark for identifying the gradient]

2 $(x - 10)(-x^2 + x + 9) = x(-x^2 + x + 9) - 10(-x^2 + x + 9)$
$= -x^3 + x^2 + 9x + 10x^2 - 10x - 90$
$= -x^3 + 11x^2 - x - 90$
[3 marks available — 1 mark for three terms correct, 1 mark for the remaining three terms correct, 1 mark for a fully correct answer with like terms collected]

3 $\dfrac{3}{5}\left(\dfrac{5}{6} - \dfrac{2}{9}\right) = \dfrac{3}{5}\left(\dfrac{15}{18} - \dfrac{4}{18}\right) = \dfrac{3}{5}\left(\dfrac{11}{18}\right) = \dfrac{33}{90} = \dfrac{11}{30}$
[2 marks available — 1 mark for correct method for subtracting fractions, 1 mark for the correct answer in its simplest form]

4 a) $\overrightarrow{XY} = \overrightarrow{XA} + \overrightarrow{AY} = -\mathbf{m} + \mathbf{n}$ or $\mathbf{n} - \mathbf{m}$ *[1 mark]*
b) $\overrightarrow{YD} = \overrightarrow{AX}$ since the squares are the same.
So $\overrightarrow{AD} = \overrightarrow{AY} + \overrightarrow{YD} = \mathbf{n} + \mathbf{m}$ *[1 mark]*
You could also use the path $\overrightarrow{AX} + \overrightarrow{XD}$.
Opposite sides in a square are parallel, so $\overrightarrow{XD} = \overrightarrow{AY} = \mathbf{n}$.

5 $g(4) = \sqrt{4} + \dfrac{1}{4} = 2 + \dfrac{1}{4} = \dfrac{9}{4}$
[2 marks available — 1 mark for substituting 4 into the function, 1 mark for the correct answer as a single fraction]

6 a) Gradient = $\dfrac{77 - 35}{10 - 24} = \dfrac{42}{-14} = -3$
$H - 77 = -3(T - 10) \Rightarrow H - 77 = -3T + 30$
$\Rightarrow H = -3T + 107$
[3 marks available — 1 mark for the correct gradient, 1 mark for using a correct formula for the equation of a line, 1 mark for the correct equation in terms of H and T with no fractions or brackets]

b) $(-3 \times 20) + 107 = -60 + 107 = 47$ tonnes *[1 mark]*

7 There is one repeated root so the discriminant is 0:
$(-6)^2 - (4 \times 1 \times c) = 0 \Rightarrow 36 - 4c = 0 \Rightarrow 4c = 36 \Rightarrow c = 9$
[3 marks available — 1 mark for identifying that discriminant is 0, 1 mark for substituting correctly into the formula for the discriminant, 1 mark for the correct answer]

8 $\dfrac{n^5 \times \sqrt{n}}{n^{\frac{3}{2}}} = n^5 \times n^{\frac{1}{2}} \times n^{-\frac{3}{2}} = n^{5 + \frac{1}{2} - \frac{3}{2}} = n^4$
[2 marks available — 1 mark for evaluating $\sqrt{n}$ as a power, 1 mark for the correct answer]

9    $W = \frac{1}{2}m(v^2 - u^2)$

$\frac{2W}{m} = v^2 - u^2$

$u^2 = v^2 - \frac{2W}{m}$

$u = \pm\sqrt{v^2 - \frac{2W}{m}}$

[3 marks available — 1 mark for multiplying by 2 and dividing by m, 1 mark for rearranging for u^2, 1 mark for the correct answer]

10   OBA = OAB = 40°

DCT = COB = OBA = 40° *(There are two sets of parallel lines so two pairs of alternate angles.)*

CDT = 90° ⇒ CTD = 180° − 90° − 40° = 50°

DTU = 90° − 50° = 40°

[3 marks available — 1 mark for the correct value of DCT, 1 mark for the correct value of CTD, 1 mark for the correct value of DTU]

11    $1 + \tan^2 x° \equiv 1 + \frac{\sin^2 x°}{\cos^2 x°} \equiv \frac{\cos^2 x° + \sin^2 x°}{\cos^2 x°} \equiv \frac{1}{\cos^2 x°}$

[2 marks available — 2 marks for a fully correct argument, otherwise 1 mark for writing $\tan^2 x°$ correctly in terms of $\sin^2 x°$ and $\cos^2 x°$]

Another correct method would be to start with the identity $\cos^2 x° + \sin^2 x° \equiv 1$ and then divide every term in it by $\cos^2 x°$.

12   Let *a* be the distance that Commuter A travels.

Commuter B travels a distance of 5*a*.

Commuter C travels a distance of *a* + 12.

Since Commuter B travels the same distance as Commuter C:

$5a = a + 12 \Rightarrow 4a = 12 \Rightarrow a = 3$

So Commuter A travels 3 km.

[3 marks available — 1 mark for correct expressions for the commuters' distances, 1 mark for setting up a correct equation with a single unknown, 1 mark for the correct final answer]

13   a) $(x + 3)(x + 12)$ or $x^2 + 15x + 36$ *[1 mark]*

     b)   Set up an equation using the information given:

$(x + 3)(x + 12) = 112 - 42$

$x^2 + 3x + 12x + 36 = 70$

$x^2 + 15x - 34 = 0$

$(x + 17)(x - 2) = 0 \Rightarrow x = -17$ or $x = 2$

But $x = -17$ would mean there are $-14 < 0$ floors.

So $x = 2$.

[4 marks available – 1 mark for setting up a correct equation, 1 mark for factorising the quadratic correctly, 1 mark for both correct solutions to the equation, 1 mark for selecting the correct answer]

14   a) $i = 5$ *[1 mark]*

$j = 360 \div 60 = 6$ *[1 mark]*

     b)   Maximum point of $y = \sin x°$ is 1,

maximum point of $y = \sin x° + k$ is 5

$\Rightarrow k = 5 - 1 = 4$ *[1 mark]*

15   Linear scale factor $= n = \frac{9}{\sqrt{6}} \div 2\sqrt{6} = \frac{9}{12} = \frac{3}{4}$

Area scale factor $= n^2 = \left(\frac{3}{4}\right)^2 = \frac{9}{16}$

Area of rectangle OABC $= 160 \times \frac{9}{16} = 10 \times 9 = 90$ cm²

Area of PQRCBA $= 160 - 90 = 70$ cm²

[4 marks available — 1 mark for the correct value of n, 1 mark for multiplying by n^2, 1 mark for the correct area of OABC, 1 mark for the correct area of PQRCBA]

It'd also be correct to use the scale factor $n = \frac{4}{3}$ — but then you'd have to divide 160 by n^2 instead of multiplying.

16   a)   The *x*- and *z*-coordinates are the same as B, so C(6, *y*, 5).

The *y*-coordinate is the side length of the square.

To find it, use Pythagoras' theorem:

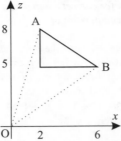

$AB^2 = (6 - 2)^2 + (8 - 5)^2 = 4^2 + 3^2 = 25 \Rightarrow AB = 5$

So C(6, 5, 5)

[3 marks available — 1 mark for both the correct x- and z-coordinates, 1 mark for using Pythagoras' theorem, 1 mark for the correct y-coordinate]

     b)   Use Pythagoras' theorem:

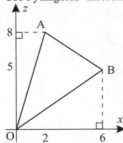

Side AB = 5 = from part a)

Side OA $= \sqrt{8^2 + 2^2} = \sqrt{68}$

Side OB $= \sqrt{6^2 + 5^2} = \sqrt{61}$

If the triangle is right-angled, OA must be the hypotenuse since this is the longest side.

$OA^2 = 68$ but $AB^2 + OB^2 = 25 + 61 = 86 \neq 68$

So the triangle is not right-angled.

[4 marks available — 1 mark for using Pythagoras' theorem to find the length of a side, 1 mark for the correct lengths of all sides, 1 mark for comparing OA^2 and $AB^2 + OB^2$, 1 mark for the correct conclusion with justification]

Practice Paper 2

1   Gradient $= \frac{8 - 2}{5 - 3} = 3$

$y - 2 = 3(x - 3) \Rightarrow y = 3x - 7$

[3 marks available — 1 mark for the correct gradient, 1 mark for using a correct method to find the equation of a line, 1 mark for the correct equation in the form $y = mx + c$]

2    $7 + 3(x - 2) < x - 11$

$7 + 3x - 6 < x - 11$

$2x < -12$

$x < -6$

[3 marks available — 1 mark for expanding brackets, 1 mark for rearranging for 2x, 1 mark for the correct answer]

3    $7t^2 - 63 = 7(t^2 - 9) = 7(t + 3)(t - 3)$

[2 marks available — 1 mark for taking out a factor of 7, 1 mark for the correct final answer]

4   Area $= \frac{1}{2}$ AB sin C so $18 = \frac{1}{2} \times 7 \times AC \times \sin 24°$

$AC = \frac{18}{\frac{1}{2} \times 7 \times \sin 24°} = 12.644... = 12.6$ cm (3 s.f.)

[3 marks available — 1 mark for correctly substituting into the formula for the area of a triangle, 1 mark for rearranging for AC, 1 mark for the correct answer]

5   a)   After 6 months, the number of deliveries made per day will be

$33 \times 1.05^6 = 44.223... = 44$

[3 marks available — 1 mark for using the multiplier 1.05, 1 mark for raising the multiplier to the power of 6, 1 mark for the correct answer]

b) $46 = 115\%$
$0.4 = 1\%$
$40 = 100\% \Rightarrow 40$ deliveries per day
[3 marks available — 1 mark for recognising that
$46 = 115\%$, 1 mark for a correct method to find 100%,
1 mark for the correct answer]

6 a) Let b be number of minutes that it takes to make the
return trip between the city and the beach and l be the
number of minutes it takes to make the return trip
between the city and the lake.
$6b + 7l = 201$ *[1 mark]*

b) $2b + 3l = 75$ *[1 mark]*

c) $2b + 3l = 75 \xrightarrow{\times 3} 6b + 9l = 225$

$\begin{array}{ll} 6b + 9l = 225 & 2b + 3l = 75 \\ \underline{6b + 7l = 201} - & 2b = 75 - (3 \times 12) \\ \quad 2l = 24 & 2b = 39 \\ \quad\quad l = 12 & \quad b = 19.5 \end{array}$

So it takes 19.5 minutes to make a return trip between the city
and the beach and 12 minutes to make a return trip between
the city and the lake.
[4 marks available — 1 mark for attempting to scale an
equation, 1 mark for a valid strategy that produces two
solutions, 1 mark for the correct values of b and l, 1 mark for
communicating the answer in minutes]

7 $134 \text{ kg} = 134\,000 \text{ g} = 1.34 \times 10^5 \text{ g}$
$(1.34 \times 10^5) \div (6.7 \times 10^{-4}) = (1.34 \div 6.7) \times (10^5 \div 10^{-4})$
$\quad\quad = 0.2 \times 10^9 = 2 \times 10^8$
[2 marks available — 1 mark for a correct method, 1 mark for
the correct answer given in scientific notation]

8 $|\mathbf{h}| = \sqrt{55^2 + 20^2 + (-1)^2} = 58.532... = 58.5$
[2 marks available — 1 mark for using Pythagoras' theorem,
1 mark for the correct answer]

9 $\dfrac{20p^2 - 5p}{q^2} \div \dfrac{5p}{9q} = \dfrac{20p^2 - 5p}{q^2} \times \dfrac{9q}{5p}$

$= \dfrac{9q(5p)(4p - 1)}{5pq^2} = \dfrac{9(4p - 1)}{q}$ or $\dfrac{36p - 9}{q}$

[3 marks available — 1 mark for turning the second fraction
upside down and multiplying, 1 mark for correctly cancelling any
term, 1 mark for the correct simplified answer]

10 $3 - 12 \sin x° = 7 \Rightarrow 12 \sin x° = -4 \Rightarrow \sin x° = -\dfrac{4}{12}$

$x = \sin^{-1}\left(-\dfrac{4}{12}\right) = -19.471...$

Since x is negative, use the C and T quadrants
in the CAST diagram.
The T quadrant gives $180 + 19.471... = 199.5$ (1 d.p.)
The C quadrant gices $360 - 19.471... = 340.5$ (1 d.p.)
[3 marks available — 1 mark for rearranging the equation
to make sin x the subject, 1 mark for one correct solution,
1 mark for the second correct solution]

11 a) In ascending order:
(258, 264, 349, 367, 394), (398, 558, 589, 745, 782)
Median $= \dfrac{394 + 398}{2} = 396$

Lower quartile $= 349$
Upper quartile $= 589$
Semi-interquartile range $= \dfrac{589 - 349}{2} = 120$

[3 marks available — 1 mark for the correct median,
1 mark for both correct quartiles, 1 mark for the correct
semi-interquartile range]

b) On average, the band sold fewer tickets as the median
was lower. The band's ticket sales were more consistent
as the semi-interquartile range was lower.
[2 marks available — 1 mark for correct comparison of
medians, 1 mark for correct comparison of
semi-interquartile ranges]

12 Using the cosine rule:
$BC^2 = 7^2 + 11^2 - 2 \times 7 \times 11 \times \cos 86° = 159.25...$
$BC = \sqrt{159.25...} = 12.619... = 12.6 \text{ km (3 s.f.)}$
[3 marks available — 1 mark for correctly substituting into the
cosine rule, 1 mark for the correct value of BC^2, 1 mark for the
correct final answer]

13 a) $f(x) = (x + 7)^2 - 3 - 7^2 = (x + 7)^2 - 52$
So $a = 7$, $b = -52$
[2 marks available — 1 mark for a, 1 mark for b]

b)
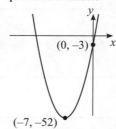
(0, –3)
(–7, –52)

[3 marks available — 1 mark for the correct coordinates of
the turning point, 1 mark for sketching a parabola with its
turning point consistent with the coordinates calculated,
1 mark for the correct y-intercept]

14 Area of sector $= \dfrac{a}{360°} \times \pi \times 6^2$ so $25 = \dfrac{36\pi a}{360°}$

$a = \dfrac{25 \times 360°}{36\pi} = 79.577... = 79.6°$ (1 d.p.)

[3 marks available — 1 mark for using the correct formula for
the area of the sector, 1 mark for rearranging to find the angle,
1 mark for the correct answer]

15 Volume of smaller cone $= \dfrac{1}{3} \times \pi \times 0.5^2 \times 1 = 0.2617... \text{ cm}^3$

Height of larger cone $= (26 \div 2) + 1 = 14$ cm

Volume of larger cone $= \dfrac{1}{3} \times \pi \times 7^2 \times 14 = 718.377... \text{ cm}^3$

Volume of half of sand timer $= 461.8... - 0.261... = 718.115... \text{ cm}^3$
Volume of sand timer $= 2 \times 718.115... = 1436.231...$
$\quad\quad = 1400 \text{ cm}^3$ (2 s.f.)

[5 marks available — 1 mark for substituting correctly into
the formula for the volume of the smaller cone, 1 mark for
substituting correctly into the formula for the volume of the
larger cone with the correct height, 1 mark for subtracting the
volumes, 1 mark for carrying out all calculations correctly,
1 mark for the correct final answer to 2 significant figures]

16 a) Using Pythagoras' theorem:
$OD^2 = 13^2 + 3^2 = 178$
$OD = \sqrt{178}$ km
[2 marks available — 1 mark for correct use of the formula
for Pythagoras' theorem, 1 mark for the correct answer]

b)
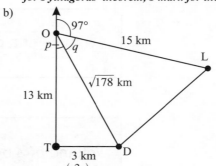

$p = \tan^{-1}\left(\dfrac{3}{13}\right) = 12.99461...$
$q = 180° - 12.99461... - 97° = 70.00538...°$
Using the cosine rule:
$DL^2 = 178 + 15^2 - 2 \times \sqrt{178} \times 15 \times \cos (70.00538...°)$
$\quad\quad = 266.1418...$
$DL = 16.313... = 16.3 \text{ km (3 s.f.)}$
[4 marks available — 1 mark for the correct value of
p, 1 mark for correct substitution into the cosine rule,
1 mark for the correct value of DL^2, 1 mark for the
correct value of DL]

Formula Sheet

There's a lot to learn for your National 5 maths exam — that's no lie. Thankfully, you'll get some formulas given to you at the start of your paper. These ones, to be precise...

The roots of $ax^2 + bx + c = 0$ are $x = \dfrac{-b \pm \sqrt{(b^2 - 4ac)}}{2a}$

Sine rule: $\dfrac{a}{\sin A} = \dfrac{b}{\sin B} = \dfrac{c}{\sin C}$

Cosine rule: $a^2 = b^2 + c^2 - 2bc \cos A$ or $\cos A = \dfrac{b^2 + c^2 - a^2}{2bc}$

Area of a triangle: $A = \dfrac{1}{2} ab \sin C$

Volume of a sphere: $V = \dfrac{4}{3} \pi r^3$

Volume of a cone: $V = \dfrac{1}{3} \pi r^2 h$

Volume of a pyramid: $V = \dfrac{1}{3} Ah$

Standard deviation: $s = \sqrt{\dfrac{\sum(x - \overline{x})^2}{n - 1}}$ or $s = \sqrt{\dfrac{\sum x^2 - \dfrac{(\sum x)^2}{n}}{n - 1}}$

(where n is the sample size)